THOMAS JEFFERSON

Champion of the People

Thomas Jefferson:

ILLUSTRATED BY ELEANOR MILL

Champion of the People

JOSEPH OLGIN

HOUGHTON MIFFLIN COMPANY

BOSTON The Riverside Press Cambridge

Contents

Library of Congress Catalog Card No. 60-13065

CHAPTER 1

Trip to Tuckahoe

On April 13, 1743, there was a great celebration on the Shadwell plantation in the Colony of Virginia. A baby boy had been born to the owners of Shadwell, Peter and Jane Jefferson.

Peter Jefferson was overjoyed. The couple already had two daughters. Now their marriage was blessed with a son and heir. "We will call him Thomas," Peter cried. "Some day he will be master of Shadwell."

Peter sent for his trusted servant Sawney. "Sawney," he said, "declare a holiday for the house servants and the field hands. I want no one to labor in the tobacco fields during the next few days."

Sawney's face crinkled into a broad grin.

"I've seen to it, Colonel, even before you told me. I've ordered extra supplies of food and the best cider for all the Shadwell people. Listen to them sing."

Peter Jefferson went to the window and watched the singing and dancing. He was a strong, kindly man. It pleased him to see his people so happy. "Good, Sawney," he said. "You may have a jug of that good cider for yourself."

Sawney chuckled. "I've taken care of that, too, Master Jefferson."

Peter smiled. "Sawney, you're a rascal. You can read my mind better than a fortune teller."

The next two years passed swiftly at Shadwell. Little Tom Jefferson grew sturdy and strong in the healthful climate of the plantation. Shadwell was located in the Piedmont (*peed'·mont*) section of central Virginia. It was called Piedmont because it was in the foothills near the mountains. On the other side of Shadwell ran the clear waters of the Rivanna River.

Tom was very happy growing up in those beautiful surroundings. However, the Jefferson family soon had to leave this beloved home.

Mrs. Jefferson's cousin, William Randolph, died. He left several young children who were unable to take care of themselves. Peter Jefferson, true to a promise he had made to William Randolph, decided to move his family to the Randolph plantation. It was called Tuckahoe, and it was sixty miles from Shadwell.

There was a great hustle and bustle as the moving day finally arrived.

"Are the children comfortable?" Peter Jefferson asked his wife. "Are they ready to leave?"

"Yes," she answered. "Jane, Mary, and baby Elizabeth will ride in the wagon with me."

"Fine," Peter said, mounting his horse. "Tom will ride on the gray mare."

"But Peter, the boy is not yet three years old. I'm afraid."

Peter laughed. "Don't worry, dear. He'll

be fine. Sawney has strapped him good and tight on a pillow. Sawney will ride the mare and hold Tom at the same time. You know how careful he is. Sawney," he called out, "take good care of our only son."

The Negro grinned as he mounted the mare. "Don't worry, Master Peter. This boy will be as safe with me as in his mammy's arms."

Tom's sister, Jane, who was almost six years old, leaped out of the wagon. She ran over to Sawney. "Don't forget to sing to Tom as you ride," she begged. "That's what I always do. He loves to hear music."

Sawney chuckled. "The birds sing much sweeter than I do, Missey Jane. They'll do the singing on this trip. My voice is so rough it would scare him."

Colonel Jefferson gave final orders. The little family started on its journey. The colonel, well over six feet tall and very strong, led the way. Behind him rode Sawney and little Tom. The wagons followed. They were filled with linen, silverware, and other neces-

sary articles. To the rear several family house-servants trotted along on horses.

At the bend of the road the party stopped and looked back. Peter dismounted. His wife left the wagon and stood beside her husband on the road. There were tears in her eyes.

"Peter," she asked, "when will we return?"

"I don't know," he said. "But it won't be before the Randolph children are able to manage their own affairs."

"It will be years before Thomas Mann Randolph will be able to, and he's the eldest boy."

"Then that is how long we will stay. Your cousin was a good man. He would have done as much for me had the good Lord taken me first."

The young woman pressed her husband's hand. "I know that, Peter. Forgive me for seeming to complain."

Peter kissed his beautiful wife. "I realize it will not be easy for you to manage two families under one roof. But Tuckahoe is a much larger plantation than Shadwell. Our family can live in one part and the Randolphs in the other."

Her mood of sadness left her. She smiled a sweet gentle smile. "Peter," she said, "my treasures are here with me. You and the children. Wherever we are together will be home to me, even if it is a log cabin in the wilderness."

The journey continued. The small red-haired boy, sitting comfortably on his pillow, was strangely silent. His hazel eyes looked in all directions. He stared curiously at the red earth of Albemarle County, Virginia. In the distance he watched the violet haze settle on the Blue Ridge Mountains. A hawk sailing in the sky above him attracted his attention. A many-colored butterfly lighted for a brief moment on the horse's back. The boy reached an eager hand to touch it. The butterfly fluttered its wings and flew away. Tom gazed after it for a long moment.

Peter Jefferson reined his horse alongside the gray mare. "Tom seems to be drinking in everything he sees," he said to Sawney.

"He's a smart boy," Sawney said. "He wants to know everything about everything. He'll be a great man some day, Master Peter."

Colonel Jefferson looked at his son with deep affection. "All fathers want to think that of their sons, Sawney. But I have a feeling that my boy is far above the ordinary. There is something unusual about him. He has such a deep curiosity. It sets him apart from all other children I have known."

The Negro slave nodded. "You're right about that, sir. Never saw a boy like Tom in my whole life."

Tom continued to enjoy the ride. It was more exciting than anything he had ever experienced before. He breathed in deeply as though the free air of Virginia were the most precious thing in the world. Everything was so beautiful — the birds singing, the purple hyacinths blooming in the fields. He knew and recognized the bluebells and the wild honeysuckle growing in the woods beside the road.

"Jane and I have picked them many times,"

he thought. Jane was his favorite sister. She had sung songs and taught him things ever since he could remember. He grew drowsy as the sun rose higher in the heavens. But he was still alert to every new bird, flower, or animal that they passed. One thing attracted him more than all the rest. As long as he could, he watched the little mountain that raised its rounded slopes across the Rivanna River. Jane had often pointed it out to him as they played in the yard at Shadwell.

"Look, Tom," she said. "Look at our beautiful mountain. Isn't it pretty?"

Mrs. Jefferson noticed Tom's great interest. "Peter," she said, "see how Tom stares at

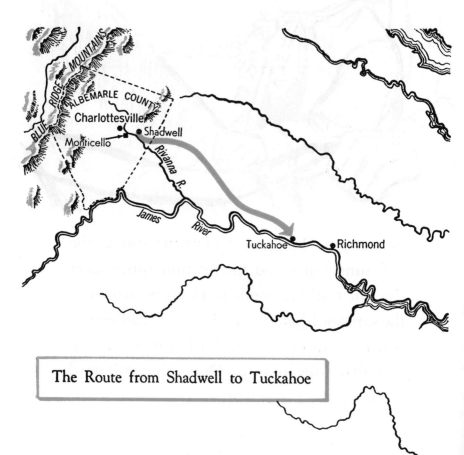

The Route from Shadwell to Tuckahoe

the mountain. He's always loved to look at that hill ever since he was a baby."

"It is different from the rest," Peter mused. "It's rounded and not as sharp or peaked. You can't blame our son for finding it so beautiful."

Tom smiled. His parents had guessed his secret. The little mountain had always fascinated him. Someday when he was older, he would go to it. He grew drowsy and slept. As he slept he dreamed of his little mountain, and he smiled again in his sleep.

Two days later, after a long, hard journey the Jefferson family reached Tuckahoe. Little Tom was sleeping. Sawney gently shook him.

"Wake up, Tom," he whispered. "Wake up and look at your new home."

CHAPTER 2

Danger in
the Wilderness

The next several years passed quickly. Young Tom grew up to be a lively, active boy of six. He was tall and strong. In the style of the day, his red hair was tied at the back of his neck.

He had a fine time at Tuckahoe. He liked to play with his sisters and cousins. Thomas Mann Randolph was his favorite cousin. That was mostly because Thomas Mann Randolph was a boy. His other two cousins were girls.

The two lads led an active life. They roamed through the fields. They watched the men tending the tobacco crops. They liked to visit the stables and the barns. They loved to jump in the hay.

Peter Jefferson taught them both to ride from the time they could sit in the saddle. But life wasn't all play for young Tom. Every weekday he attended the little white schoolhouse Peter Jefferson had built in the yard. His sisters and cousins also went to the same school. Peter had promised William Randolph that he would see that the Randolph children received a good education.

The schoolmaster was a young man just over from England. He taught the boys and girls to read, write, and figure. Tom liked to go to school. He was a fine pupil. His father was delighted with Tom's progress.

"Tom has a natural ability for schoolwork," the teacher said. "He can write his name better than any of the other pupils."

Thomas Mann Randolph sniffed. "No wonder, he's always practicing and studying. The other day he wrote his name on a slate over a hundred times."

20

"Perhaps you should do the same," Peter Jefferson added dryly.

Peter was away from Tuckahoe a great deal of the time. He was busy surveying the wild, distant parts of the frontier. It was dangerous, exciting work. How Tom wished he were old enough to go with his father! He begged Peter to take him along on one of the trips.

Peter's eyes twinkled. "You're hardly big enough to make a mouthful for one of those huge timber wolves. When you have more meat on your bones, I might take you."

Whenever Peter Jefferson went on a surveying trip, the boys waited impatiently for his return. Although Mrs. Jefferson tried not to show it, Tom knew she was often worried.

"Father will be all right," he said to comfort her. "Nothing will happen to him. He's too strong and powerful."

"You're a fine, considerate boy to comfort me," his mother smiled. But inwardly she shuddered as she thought of the savage Indians and the wild frontier that her husband was surveying.

One job that the governor asked Peter Jefferson to do was the most dangerous of all. He and Joshua Fry, a former professor from the College of William and Mary, went out with a party of men to map the Virginia-North Carolina border. Part of the work had to be done in the wild western land beyond the Blue Ridge Mountains. No man had ever surveyed that rugged country.

The men were gone so long that everyone at Tuckahoe became worried. Tom could hardly keep his attention on his work at school. Anxious weeks went by and still no word came.

One morning in particular seemed to move more slowly than all the others. Through the open schoolhouse window Tom could see the sunlight bathing the trees. A blue jay flew by, chattering gaily. A bee, busy with its work of gathering honey, buzzed by. Tom tried to concentrate on his school work, but he couldn't. He suddenly sniffed. A wonderful aroma from the kitchen reached his nostrils. He was so hungry. Why hadn't he eaten more for breakfast? Oh, yes, he'd been thinking of his father. He had passed up the delicious hominy grits that Dulcy, the cook, had prepared. He hadn't eaten the hot pancakes either. The wind brought him more and more delicious odors. He tightened his belt.

"Dulcy must be roasting beef," he whispered to Nancy.

"Idle talk is for idle minds," the schoolmaster roared. He was very strict.

Tom tried to forget his hunger. He tried to think about his lessons. He couldn't do it. He could only think of the delicious meat Dulcy was roasting. His mouth watered. He wondered what time it was, but he didn't dare ask the teacher. Oh, if time could only go faster, then lunch would come sooner. He began to pray quietly to himself. That might make lunch come quicker. He repeated the Lord's Prayer over and over again. Sure enough, in a few moments the schoolmaster called out, "Everyone will go home for lunch. Be back promptly, as lateness and loitering will lead you down the wrong path."

Tom fairly flew to the big house. He was the first at the table and the last to leave.

"My gracious," his mother declared. "I've never seen a youngster eat so much before. You'd better stop, Tom, before you burst."

But Tom was too busy eating to say anything. He wondered if his prayers had actually made time go faster, or if it only seemed so. Just as he was ready to go back to school, Sawney arrived. Tom was shocked when he saw how worn, tired, and thin his father's faithful servant looked.

"Where's Father?" he asked.

Sawney had been one of the men who had set out to work on the Virginia-North Carolina line. Before he could answer, Mrs. Jefferson and all the children were bombarding Sawney with questions.

"Is Colonel Jefferson safe?" his wife asked.

"Did you see any wild Indians?" sister Jane wanted to know.

"The master is alive and safe," Sawney gasped. But he was too weak to say any more.

Mrs. Jefferson quickly tended to him. Like most of the other Virginia women, she was trained in nursing. After he had eaten and felt better, Sawney told his story.

"The country Colonel Jefferson is surveying is the wildest I've ever seen. There are dismal swamps, and we lost many of our horses. The colonel saved several men from drowning. The mountain ridges come one after another. Each ridge is higher than the one before it. They never seem to stop."

25

Tom tried to imagine what the mountains looked like in the wilderness. He suddenly remembered his own little mountain back at Shadwell. It had been such a long time ago, but he still remembered it.

"And the wolves," Sawney shuddered. "They were bigger and fiercer than I ever saw before. At night we slept in trees in order to be safe. We tied ourselves to the branches so we wouldn't fall out."

"What about the horses?" Thomas Mann Randolph asked. "Were they all right?"

"Yes, we built huge fires around them. The wolves were afraid to attack. They fear fire."

"Why did you come back alone?" Mrs. Jefferson asked.

"Because the colonel made me. Most of the other men and I became sick with fever. The colonel ordered me to come back."

"Is he ill?" Jane asked anxiously.

"Not the colonel. And if he were, he wouldn't show it. He cheered us up even when we had to shiver without a fire and eat raw meat."

"We tied ourselves to the branches. . ."

"Why was that?" Tom interrupted.

"Because we didn't dare light a campfire. There was a band of wild Indians in the near-by forest. The only good thing about that was that the Indians frightened away the wolves."

"One day a bear killed my pet horse," Sawney continued.

"What did you do with the horse?" Thomas Mann Randolph inquired.

"We had horse meat for supper. We had lost all our food while crossing a raging river. We were starving. We didn't dare shoot at game because of the savages."

Tom's sisters looked frightened. But Tom felt a warm pride in his father. Of all the men, his father was the strongest and best leader. Some day he hoped he could be like him.

Sawney finished the story by saying, "If any man can map the line, it will be Colonel Jefferson. But I'm afraid it can't be done by human flesh and blood."

Tom suddenly remembered the Lord's Prayer. This time he prayed for an important thing, his father's safety and success.

A week later a mighty shout went up from the plantation workers. Colonel Jefferson, Joshua Fry, and some of the other men had returned. Tom rushed into his father's arms as soon as he could. Peter Jefferson was worn and haggard, but he had a proud light in his eyes.

"We drew the line, Son," he said waving a folded paper. "We mapped it at last!"

Mrs. Jefferson's eyes grew misty. "Oh Peter," she cried, "who cares about a piece of paper? It's you we were worried about!"

CHAPTER 3

Feats of Strength

The following morning Peter Jefferson was up bright and early. He mounted his horse and inspected the plantation just as though nothing had happened. Tom and Thomas Mann Randolph rode along with him. They visited one of the tobacco barns. The rich smell of aging tobacco was pleasant to Tom's nostrils.

The tobacco was being cured. Young Thomas had first watched the plants growing in the fields. The men had cut the green tobacco leaves and taken them to the barn to be dried and aged. Now that the tobacco leaves had turned brown, they were packed in huge thousand-pound barrels called hogsheads. Several of the men were trying to stand two hogsheads of tobacco upright. When the hogsheads stood upright, they left more room for storage. No matter how the Negroes tugged and strained, they couldn't stand the hogsheads in an erect position.

The overseer was annoyed. "We'll have to get more men to help us," he said.

Peter Jefferson smiled. "I don't think so. The men are busy at other tasks. Let me try."

Tom's eyes almost bulged from their sockets as Peter stood between the two huge barrels of tobacco. Was his father going to attempt to stand both up at once? Peter had tremendous strength, but this was over two thousand pounds.

"He'll never be able to do it," Thomas Mann Randolph whispered.

"I'm sure he will," Tom said. He was fiercely loyal to his father.

Slowly, ever so slowly, Peter Jefferson raised both hogsheads to a standing position. Tom clapped and cheered. He felt the hard muscles in his father's arms.

"Look, Thomas Mann," he called proudly. "Look at the most powerful muscles in the whole world."

"Hardly that," Peter smiled. "There are many strong men in Virginia. I met a young surveyor in the wilderness called George Washington. He is the strongest man I ever saw."

A little farther on they met several of the workers trying to push down a deserted shed. But in spite of their efforts, the shed would not budge.

"I couldn't spare more men for this task either," the overseer apologized. "We're behind in our shipments to the market."

Before he realized it, Tom blurted out, "My father can push the shed down by himself." As soon as the words left his mouth, he was sorry he said them.

Thomas Mann Randolph looked doubtful. "I don't think so, Tom," he whispered. "Nobody can be that strong."

"Stand aside," Peter Jefferson said to the men. He leaned against the side of the shed.

He looked at Tom and winked. "What my son thinks I can do, I must try to accomplish."

Tom almost burst out crying. He wished that he could take back his words. He didn't want his father to fail in front of the others.

Colonel Jefferson seemed to read his son's mind. "It's no disgrace to fail in an honest attempt," he said. "The only disgrace is to be afraid to try a difficult task." He pushed and strained. Nothing happened.

Tom closed his eyes. He didn't want to see his father fail. Then he heard a little creak. He opened his eyes. Was he seeing things, or did the shed move a little? It creaked some more and shifted a trifle. Then before you could say "King George," the shed crashed to the ground!

Tom's chest puffed out. "See, Thomas Mann Randolph," he boasted proudly. "I told you my father could do it."

His cousin grinned sheepishly. "Sure," he said. "I knew he could do it, too. I was only teasing you."

CHAPTER 4

Alone on
the Mountain

When Tom was nine years old, Peter Jefferson decided to move his family back to Shadwell. He had kept his promise to his dead friend and relative. Tuckahoe had been well taken care of during the seven years the Jeffersons lived there. The Randolph children were well and happy. Thomas Mann Randolph was on his way to a good education. A faithful overseer was in charge of the plantation.

Tom was sad as he said good-by to his cousins. "I'll never forget you," he whispered to Thomas Mann Randolph. "You'll always be like a brother to me."

However, the excitement of exploring Shadwell all over again soon made him forget about Tuckahoe. Shadwell was in much wilder country than Tuckahoe. It had been named after the section of London where Tom's mother was born. Tom liked the life at Shadwell better than at Tuckahoe. The neighbors weren't as fine and fancy, but they were good friendly people. They were more independent than the aristocrats who lived in the older Tidewater parts of Virginia. The Tidewater people were called that because they lived on the rivers near the coast.

Tom was delighted with his little mountain. "It's just as I remembered it in my dreams," he told his father. "On a spring day it's beautiful with the redbud and dogwood trees in blossom."

Peter Jefferson was pleased. "I'm glad you have so much love for the land, Tom. Some day Shadwell will be yours. I know you'll take good care of it. It's smaller than Tuckahoe, but in my opinion more beautiful."

"It is, Father," Tom cried. "To me it's more beautiful than the grandest house in all Virginia. I do not measure the value of a home by its size."

Peter Jefferson nodded. "That's fine. Nor should you value a person more because of his high position, title, or money."

"I will never do that," Tom said. "I notice that you treat all men equally. It doesn't matter to you whether they are rough men of your surveying party or grand gentlemen from the Tidewater."

Peter chuckled. "I'll tell you a secret, Tom. I have found the so-called rough men better friends than the aristocrats sent by the King of England to govern us. The common man is more to be depended upon."

Tom's hazel eyes widened. "I'll never forget that," he said. And he never did.

Colonel Jefferson was very busy. He was the county surveyor, a justice of the peace, and a colonel of the militia. He was also a member of the House of Burgesses and helped make the laws for the colony. Yet he spent as much time as he could with Tom. He taught him how to hunt in the mountains near Shadwell. He taught him how to swim in the Rivanna River.

"It's important to be able to swim," he said. "Besides being wonderful exercise, it can often save your life."

"I remember Sawney telling us how you saved some of your men from drowning," Tom said. "I'll learn to be a good swimmer."

One hot, summer evening, Peter spoke to his son. "Tom," he said, "tomorrow morning I want you to go alone to your little mountain. Take your gun. Spend the day hunting there with no companions. It will teach you to depend on just yourself."

"But Peter," Tom's mother protested. "Tom is only ten years old. He's too young."

"Nonsense," Peter laughed. "He needs to get away from his five sisters now and then. I want him to grow up manly and brave."

"Tom will probably be afraid to go," his sister Mary laughed. Some of the others joined in.

"Be quiet, all of you," Jane snapped. As usual, she stood up for Tom. "I'm sure Tom will do us proud."

"We'll see," Mary mocked with an I-told-you-so manner.

Tom could hardly sleep that night. He had never been to the mountain alone. He had never gone hunting by himself. He hoped he wouldn't be afraid as his sister Mary seemed to think. He clenched his fists. No, no matter what, he wouldn't be a coward and return empty-handed.

The next morning after a hearty breakfast, he set out on his adventures. He waded across the Rivanna. Then he started the steep climb through the woods to the top of his little mountain. Squirrels and rabbits scurried out of his path. He saw a deer in the underbrush, but it ran away. He looked back. How far away Shadwell seemed! If anything happened, if he needed help, no one would hear him call. Suppose he met a wild buffalo. He set his jaw firmly. He wouldn't call for help, even if he saw a wolf. Wolves were

41

a great source of danger and nuisance in the county. They killed lambs, calves, chickens, and other livestock. They even attacked humans sometimes. The plantation owners offered seventy pounds of tobacco for killing a young wolf. They gave a hundred and forty pounds of tobacco for an old one.

As the day wore on, Tom became discouraged. He wasn't skillful enough to catch the squirrels and rabbits. They all ran at his approach. He didn't get a single shot. He received a bad scare when he almost stepped on a rattlesnake. The poisonous creature hissed and glided away. Tom wiped the sweat off his brow with a sigh of relief.

He lay down to rest in a clearing. What a beautiful view! To the west he could see the Southwestern Mountains. His father had surveyed much of that area. Right behind Tom's mountain was a higher one. It was called Peter's Mountain, after his father. He wondered if he would ever be famous enough to have a mountain named after him. "Will I ever have the strength of body and

character my father has?" Tom thought.

Peter Jefferson was held in great respect. Tom had heard Dr. Thomas Walker, their nearest neighbor, tell John Harvie, another Albemarle planter, that Peter Jefferson was the country's most important citizen. Tom had often heard his elders talk about his father's sense of duty. "No one else would have given up his own lands to take care of a friend's plantation for seven years the way Peter Jefferson had," they said.

Tom jumped to his feet. "I'd better stop daydreaming and do something before I disgrace the name of Jefferson."

As he tramped along the woods he suddenly heard a loud "gobble, gobble, gobble." It was a wild turkey. Here was his chance. Quietly, ever so quietly, he tip-toed into position for a good shot. The turkey was sitting in the branches of a tall tree. It was a hard shot even for a man, and he was only a boy. He'd never hit it. Then he squared his shoulders and took aim. He held his rifle steady as his father had taught him and squeezed the trigger. Bang! It was a perfect shot. He left the bird lying in the clearing and entered the underbrush. His luck had changed. Now he was after more game. He had gone only a few hundred feet when he heard something that brought him to a dead halt. He quickly retraced his steps. His heart almost stopped beating as he burst into the clearing. There, ready to pounce upon Tom's turkey, was a big gray wolf. Tom was so angry that he yelled, "Hey, that's my turkey. Leave it alone."

The wolf turned and snarled at him. Tom's knees began shaking. The beast glared at the boy with blood-shot eyes. Saliva dripped from its mouth. Tom's lips moved in prayer as he raised his musket. If he missed this shot, he'd be done for. Before he could shoot again the wolf would tear him to pieces. He tried to hold his gun steady. The wolf crouched to spring. Tom shifted the gun until he could see the killer squarely in the sights. Bang! The mountainside echoed and re-echoed with the roar of the shot. The

wolf was stopped in mid-air just as he charged. He would no more be a menace to the people and livestock of Albemarle County.

Tom suddenly became weak in the knees, and he had to sit down. He felt faint. After a while he felt better. He walked over to the turkey and slung it over his back. "This day should make me famous," he muttered. "A young, luscious turkey and an old wolf, both in five minutes. Wait till Father sees the size of this wolf. He'll be proud of me, and so will Jane. "I'm so glad I didn't disappoint them."

CHAPTER 5

The Big Buffalo

A short time after Tom's successful solo hunt, his father arranged for him to go to the school of Parson William Douglas. The minister lived some distance from Shadwell. Tom boarded there all week. He came home only on week ends. He missed Shadwell, but he realized his education must come first. He studied French, Latin, and Greek at the school. Only a few boys attended the Douglas School. Education was not open to everyone. Only the sons of the rich gentlemen planters who could afford to pay had a chance to go to school.

Tom did not like this. "I think everyone in the colony should have a chance for an education," he told his father.

Peter agreed. "Everyone should have an equal opportunity, Tom, but it will take a long time for people to agree to that. I have mentioned this to some of my friends. But the planters say it would be too expensive."

Tom shook his head. "The cost of education would be worth the price. Look at all the money the Reverend Mr. Robert Rose has saved our planters. He taught them to lash two canoes together. Now they can ship hogsheads of tobacco down the river to the market without the danger of the canoes tipping. If Parson Rose hadn't been well-educated, he might never have thought of the plan. Think of all the other wonderful things educated men might invent."

Peter chuckled. "Tom, if you ever get elected to public office, those who oppose education for all will be in for a rough time."

Tom smiled grimly. "I think they will, Father."

Peter patted his son on the back. "Good. I approve of intelligent opposition to authority. Always remember you are descended from English yeomen (*yoh' · men*). They value the right of freedom and free speech above life itself."

Tom looked at his father with great interest. "Mother told me the same thing. Just exactly what was a yeoman?"

"Well, Son, the English yeoman was a small farmer. He owned a plot of land which he worked himself. It might have been a very poor piece of property. He might have lived in a tumble-down hut. But even the King of England could not cross over the threshold without the yeoman's permission."

Tom's eyes sparkled. "I'm glad my ancestors were yeomen. I admire such independence."

"That wasn't all, Tom. The yeomen could not be punished or put in jail without a trial by jury. They may have lived a poorer life than the great lords and ladies, but they were fiercely jealous of their right to be free."

Tom looked up at his little mountain and breathed in deeply. He looked at the slaves

51

laboring in the fields and frowned. "Father," he said, "some day all men may be free."

"That may take many years, Tom," his father said. "But I believe it will come."

"I know it will," Tom said quietly.

The elder Jefferson stared. He had never heard Tom speak so intensely about anything before.

That night a tribe of Indians camped on the ground of Shadwell. They lit their camp-fires near the Rivanna River.

"Come, Tom," Peter said. "I want you to meet my friend the great Cherokee chief, On-tassete *(on' · tah · seh' · tee)*."

The Cherokees were very happy to see Colonel Jefferson. Of all the white men, they loved and trusted Peter most. They always camped on his land when they traveled to Williamsburg to discuss treaties with the government.

"Welcome to our fire," Chief Ontassete said in English. He shook Tom's hand warmly. "A special welcome to the son of my old friend."

Tom was thrilled as he sat cross-legged around the fire with the Cherokees. There was a full moon which made it almost as light as day. He watched wide-eyed as his father puffed the peace pipe with the Indians.

The chief was a huge man. He appeared seven feet tall. His coppery skin gleamed as the fire rose higher. The chief spoke to his braves in the musical Cherokee language. Although Tom didn't understand the words, he listened spellbound.

"Ontassete is a wonderful speaker," he whispered to his father. "He reminds me of the great Greek orators I am learning about from Parson Douglas."

"He is without doubt a splendid speaker," Peter answered. "Some day he plans to get permission to visit the King of England."

"What will he do in England?" Tom asked.

"He wants to tell the King about the unfair treatment the white man has given his people."

"Will the King listen to him?"

"I don't know, Son. But Ontassete is right.

It is shameful how the white man has stolen the red man's lands and broken solemn treaties."

Ontassete arose and stretched his powerful arms toward the moon. His seamed face was grave and earnest as he prayed to the Great Spirit.

Tom felt sad. A deep pity for the Indians welled up inside him. Perhaps some day, when he grew up, he could help them. One thing he knew, he would always treat them kindly and befriend them just as his father did.

Ontassete spoke. "We will now have a dance in honor of our young visitor." The braves arose and danced in a circle around the fire. They chanted songs as they danced. The waters of the Rivanna sparkled in the moonlight. The Indians whirled and leaped faster and faster.

"I shall never forget this night," Tom muttered. "Everything is so beautiful. It seems like a dream."

When the dancing was finished, Peter

wanted to take Tom home. "It's late, Son," he said. "It's time you were sleeping."

"Please let me stay, Father," Tom begged. "A brave told me Ontassete always ends a campfire with a story."

"Let the young one listen to my tale," Ontassete requested.

Everyone grew silent as the chief began his story. "Once many, many moons ago, our tribe was in great danger. Down from the north came the big buffaloes. They were bigger than young trees. The ground trembled with their heavy footsteps. They were fierce and terrible. They killed and ate our deer and other game animals. The Cherokees were starving."

"Why didn't the Cherokees kill the big buffaloes?" Tom asked.

"Because, young one, the big buffaloes were too strong and powerful. Arrows could not pierce their thick skins. Spears would break into splinters when they hit their hard bodies. The Cherokees were helpless. The medicine men prayed to the Great Spirit.

56

The Great Spirit heard and answered their
prayers. He seated himself on a mountain.
He hurled lightning bolts at the monsters.
He killed all of them except the great bull.
The bull caught the bolts on his gigantic
horns. His head was so hard that the bolts
could not harm him. The Great Spirit tried
again. This time a lightning bolt hit the big
buffalo in the side. He was badly wounded

and frightened, so he ran way. He leaped over the Ohio River, the Wabash, and the Illinois. Finally, he bounded over the Great Lakes where he is still living to this day."

Tom was fascinated by the story. "Was there really a big buffalo, Ontassete?" he asked.

The chief nodded. "I have seen the proof."

"What was that?" Peter asked.

"I have found some of their great bones during my hunting trips through the West."

"Perhaps they were bones of a bear or a present-day buffalo," Tom suggested.

"No, my son, these bones were many times larger than the biggest animals we have living in our country today. Besides, once in a cave hidden in the mountains, I came upon a picture of the animal. It had been drawn by one of our ancient ancestors. A mighty bear, also drawn in the picture, looked like a little dwarf next to the big buffalo."

Tom became excited. "There's a big Indian mound farther up the river. Perhaps there I can find the bones of such a creature."

Ontassete smiled. "I do not think so, my son."

Tom wasn't sleepy even on the way home. He couldn't get the story of the big buffalo out of his mind. "Do you believe there was such an animal, Father?"

"Yes," Peter Jefferson said. "I have heard Professor Fry speak about it on our surveying trips. He said it looked like an elephant, only it was much larger and fiercer. I believe he called it a mammoth."

Tom's eyes shone. "Some day I would like to go to the College of William and Mary. I would like to learn about such wonderful things of the past."

"You will go, Son. I promise you that."

When Tom went to bed that night, he couldn't sleep a wink. In the morning he would take his servant, Jupiter, and dig in the Indian mound. Maybe he could find the bones of a huge, strange animal that looked like an elephant. Such a discovery would make him famous. He fell asleep smiling at the wonderful thought.

CHAPTER 6

The Indian Mound

Just as dawn broke, Tom went down to the slaves' quarters and called Jupiter. Jupiter, a husky boy about Tom's age, wasn't anxious to go digging in the Indian mound.

"Master Tom," he said, "I heard say there are ghosts in that pile."

Tom laughed. "There are no such things as ghosts."

"I-I don't know," Jupiter stammered. "They say the mound is full of Indians that were killed in a big battle many years ago. Some of their spirits might still be hanging around."

But Tom was firm. "Get the tools, Jupiter. I'll get the canoe ready."

"Can't we ride there on horseback, Master Tom? We can leave quicker if we have to."

Tom chuckled. "If we have to leave that fast, we'll be safer on the Rivanna. If there are such things as ghosts, I've never heard of one that could swim."

The canoe ride was enjoyable. The water was clear and cool. The gentle breeze from the mountains was refreshing. Birds sang in the nearby trees.

But Tom, who usually loved to observe nature, could think of only one thing — the bones of the big buffalo. If they could only find some, it would prove that the big creatures once lived and roamed the woods and meadows near Shadwell.

Soon they reached the Indian mound on the banks of the river. They began to dig. Tom dug with great energy. Jupiter dug quite gingerly. They dug five deep holes and found nothing. Jupiter's spirits rose.

"This is just an empty mound," he said. "There never were any Indians buried here."

62

Tom wiped the sweat off his brow. "I'm not quitting until I find something." He began to dig in another section of the mound. Suddenly his shovel hit something. "Jupiter!" he yelled. "I've struck something hard!"

"M-might be a stone," Jupiter stammered.

"I don't think so," Tom said. He got down on his knees and felt at the bottom of the hole. Gently, so as not to break it, he slowly pulled out a human bone. "It's an arm bone," Tom gasped. "We studied the human skeleton from a book in Parson Douglas' library."

Jupiter was scared. "Let's get out of here, Tom. The ghosts of those old Indians won't like having their bones disturbed."

"I'm just starting to dig," Tom said. The shovel unearthed more and more bones. They were of all sizes and shapes. They were all mixed together: leg bones, arm bones, and back bones. One thing puzzled Tom. They weren't arranged in any order. They should have been, if warriors killed in battle had been buried there. "Jupiter," he said, "these

63

bones were brought here from another place and dumped. There's nothing to worry about. These Indians died far from here. Then after a long while their bones were buried in the mound."

"I feel better now," Jupiter said. "They say ghosts only haunt the spot where they were killed."

A little farther down Tom found the skull of a baby. "This skull completely destroys the legend that there was a battle here."

Jupiter grinned. "You know, Master Tom," he said, "you and I will be able to prove that some of the folks around here are big liars. Let's stop now. We can take a swim and do some fishing."

"No," Tom grunted stubbornly. "I'm going to find what I came for — the bones of a big buffalo."

The boys dug all afternoon. They found hundreds of other bones, but none were large enough to have belonged to the big animal they were seeking.

Tom was disappointed. He finally called

a halt. "All right, Jupiter," he sighed. "Let's pile all the bones neatly in the baskets."

"What good are old bones?" Jupiter asked.

"I'm going to have father bring them to the professors at the College of William and Mary."

"What do they want with old bones?"

"They may add to some of the knowledge already known of Indian customs," Tom said. "If that is so, our hard work will be worthwhile."

"How about the big buffaloes? Are we going to look other places for them?"

"No, Jupiter. I have to go back to school tomorrow. But this I promise you. Some day I'll learn all about the big buffaloes. Some day I'll find their bones. Then people all over the colonies, not only professors, will realize that there is a great deal of truth in the old Indian legends."

Tom went back to school and devoted himself full time to his studies. He wanted to learn everything he could, not only about the present, but also about the past. He was fascinated with the knowledge of the ancient Greeks and Romans. "Their civilization was much higher than ours," he thought. "We can learn from them."

The boys at the Douglas School heard many stories of the troubles with the French and Indians. The French were stirring up the Indians against the English settlers. The boys were shocked when they heard the terrible news of how the Indians massacred General Braddock's troops. The General had tried to fight the Indians in the European fashion. He ignored the advice of George Washington, who was one of his officers, to fight from cover, as the Indians did. The Indians hid behind rocks and trees. They destroyed the English army from ambush.

One thing that cheered up the boys was the heroism of George Washington. The gallant Virginian had two horses shot from under him, yet he rallied the beaten soldiers and led an orderly retreat. If it hadn't been for Washington, the slaughter would have been worse.

Although the fighting was on the western frontier quite a distance from Shadwell, Tom was worried about his father. Colonel Jefferson was busy drilling his militia. He wanted to be ready in case the Indians raided Albemarle County.

One week end when Tom was fourteen years old, he found his father at home. The Colonel looked pale and tired.

"Father," he begged. "Why don't you take a rest. Looking after the plantation, acting as a justice of the peace, and drilling your troops is too much for even your great strength."

Peter Jefferson shook his head. "It is my duty to do everything I can to defend the valley. Besides, I'm not old yet."

Tom sighed. He realized his father would never shirk any of his duties.

☆　　☆　　☆

One day Parson Douglas sent for him. "You must go home at once, Tom," he said.

"Is anything wrong with Father?" Tom asked.

"Is anything wrong with Father?"

"Yes, hurry."

Tom rode his horse hard. He leaped from the panting animal's back as soon as they reached Shadwell. He ran all the way to the house. One glance and he knew he was too late. Everyone was in tears. He rushed into his father's bedroom. Dr. Walker was there.

"Father!" Tom cried.

Dr. Walker gently took his hand. "Tom," he said, "your father is dead. But his last words were to tell you not to worry. He said you were the man of the house now. You will have to take good care of your mother, sisters, and brother."

"I will," Tom murmured, choking back his tears. "I'll come home from school for good."

"No, Tom," Dr. Walker said. "Your father wanted you to continue your education. He said you were to go to the Reverend Mr. Maury's school. After that you must go to college."

"What about my duty to my family?"

"He said you could serve them better later on, if you first received a good education."

"I will follow my father's wishes. I'll study everything I can and become a well-educated man. Somewhere, somehow, Father will know about it and be glad."

CHAPTER 7

Boarding School

Tom stayed at Shadwell for several months after his father's death. He cheered and comforted his mother. He took care of his sisters and his brother Randolph. Even though only fourteen years old, he helped manage the estate. He kept records of the finances and tobacco crops. He made a habit of writing down important things in separate notebooks. Then if he needed to know something, all he had to do was to look it up. This habit of keeping notes stayed with him all his life.

Finally, when things were well organized, he turned over the management of Shadwell to a trusted overseer. He was now ready to go to Reverend James Maury's school.

Tom was delighted with his new school.

Reverend Maury was a wonderful teacher. The school was held in a large cabin which was fourteen miles from Shadwell. Tom boarded in the Maury household with a few other pupils. Reverend Maury had twelve children of his own, so there was never a dull moment at meals or any other time.

Tom became close friends with Matthew Maury, the son of Reverend Maury nearest Tom's own age. He often took Matthew home with him to Shadwell for week-end visits. But the boy he liked best at school was Dabney Carr. Dabney was six months younger than Tom. He came from a large family of thirteen children. Luckily, his parents believed in education. They scraped and saved so Dabney could go to school.

Reverend Maury charged his pupils twenty-two pounds a year. Tom once wrote that it was the best bargain he ever got. The teacher not only knew Latin, Greek, and French thoroughly, but he was a born leader. He inspired Tom to study English literature, religion, and philosophy, also. Tom took to his studies like a fish to water. Reverend Maury soon saw that Tom had an unusual mind.

"Tom," he said, "don't be like some pupils I've had. Don't stop learning when you're about twenty years old."

"I won't," Tom said. "I'll never stop studying. I'll be a student all my life."

But schoolwork wasn't all that occupied Tom's time. On his mother's insistence he learned dancing. Whenever he and Dabney came home on vacations, Mr. Ingles, the dancing master, was there. The Jefferson girls, of course, also joined in the lessons. Tom wasn't enthusiastic about dancing at first. He complained to his mother that it was a waste of time.

"Nonsense, Tom," she said. "A Virginia gentleman should know something about the social graces, too."

Tom smiled. His mother knew that he cared little for social things. Like his father, Tom was a man of the common people.

Tom also learned to play the violin. He

loved music. His sister Jane played the harpsichord. They spent many happy hours playing classical duets. Jane had a fine voice, and she sang hymns and psalms as she played. Tom always liked the psalms best. The brother and sister livened up Shadwell with their music.

One day Tom showed Dabney his mountain. The two boys spent the day hunting along its slopes. Tom didn't try to kill anything. He was more interested in observing the habits of the animals and how they lived. Finally, tired, they stopped to rest under a huge oak tree.

"Some day," Tom said, "I will build a grand house up here."

Dabney shrugged his shoulders. "It's a foolish idea, Tom. People don't build houses on mountains. Everyone knows the best place to build a house is by a river."

Tom set his jaws stubbornly. "I will be different," he said. "Although my mountain is small, it has a large view. Come, Dabney, let's climb this tree. I'll show you."

The boys climbed the tree and sat down on a thick branch. Even Dabney was impressed by the surrounding countryside.

"Why, you can see the Blue Ridge Mountains clearly from here, Tom. And on the other side it seems as if you are looking at all Virginia. It's beautiful."

Tom was happy that his friend liked his mountain.

"But," continued Dabney, "how will you get the building materials up here?"

"I'll build a road," Tom said. His hazel eyes brightened as he thought of the future of his mountain.

Dabney was impressed. "You know, Tom," he said, "I believe you'll accomplish your dream some day. Tell you what — let's make a vow."

"What shall it be?" Tom asked.

"Well," Dabney said seriously, "let's agree that when we die, we'll both be buried here on the mountain."

"Agreed," Tom said. And the friends shook hands.

But although Tom and Dabney were fast friends, they sometimes had disagreements. Back at school they argued about whose horse would win in a race. Tom secretly knew Dabney's horse could beat his pony, but he wouldn't admit it. One winter's day he accepted Dabney's challenge.

"All right, Dabney," he said. "I'll race you the thirtieth day of this month."

Dabney trained his horse all during the month. He practiced racing him even when it snowed. Tom appeared unconcerned and made no special training for the race.

"You'll lose by a big distance if you don't get down to business soon," Matthew Maury warned.

Tom's eyes twinkled. "I don't think so."

Finally after the twenty-eighth day of the month, the boys discovered Tom's hoax.

"Dabney, you can't race Tom the thirtieth day of February," they said, rolling in merriment. "There is no thirtieth day of February."

Dabney took Tom's joke good-naturedly. The race between the fast horse and the slow pony never did come off.

A few days later Dabney Carr and the grown-up Jefferson children went to a house party at the home of Colonel Dandridge. Tom took his violin along.

"I'll play for some of the dances," he said. After he arrived he was glad he had learned to dance. The young ladies at the party all complimented Tom on his ability.

"That's due to my mother," Tom thought. "I'll always be grateful to her for this accomplishment." He was playing a lively tune for the Virginia reel when a young man entered. He was older than Tom, and his clothes were rather poor and shabby. Tom looked down on his own lace ruffles and neatly pressed satin suit. He touched his powdered wig.

"I hope the seedy stranger gets a good welcome here," he thought. "He looks out of place."

To Tom's surprise, everyone was glad to see the newcomer, Patrick Henry. The young ladies flocked around him. Tom's eyes widened in surprise. He soon found out the reason for the young man's popularity. He was a wonderful speaker. There was something about his voice that held one spell-

bound. Patrick Henry had a ready wit, too. He soon had everyone laughing at his jokes.

Tom, who wasn't a good speaker, felt a little envious. "I wish I could talk like him," he thought.

But the newcomer soon made Tom like him. "Let's play some tunes together," he said. "I could play either my flute or my violin in a duet with you."

Patrick Henry turned out to be a fine player. He and Tom became so interested in their music that they didn't notice how fast time flew. Finally, two pretty young ladies made them stop.

"Playing is fine," they pouted, "but we came here to dance."

Tom and Patrick laughed and joined the girls in a lively reel.

On the way home Tom confided in Dabney. "I like that Patrick Henry," he said. "I've a feeling that I'll get to know him better later on."

Tom spent two happy years at the Reverend Mr. Maury's school. One day the teacher

sent for him. "Tom," he said, "I have taught you everything I know. It's time for you to seek further help in your education. You are almost seventeen. I think you should go to college."

"William and Mary?" Tom asked.

Parson Maury nodded. "Yes. There is an exceptionally fine teacher there, a Mr. William Small. He has a wonderful scientific mind. You could learn much from him."

On the way home to Shadwell, Tom stopped in at Colonel Peter Randolph's house. The colonel was not only a relative, but he was also one of the men in charge of the Jefferson estate. Tom told him of his wish to go to William and Mary. The older man agreed that it would be a wise thing. "It is what your father would have wanted," he said.

Tom arrived at Shadwell and wrote a letter about going to William and Mary to his other guardian, John Harvie. He waited impatiently for an answer. It finally came. John Harvie was also in agreement. Tom was overjoyed. He could now learn all the wonderful things that a college could teach him.

"I shall study history, architecture, philosophy, religion, and mathematics," he thought. "All these things I must learn and many more, too. I shall fulfill my duty to my family, my friends, and to the people of Virginia. My father wanted all this for me. I shall not fail him."

Then a sweet, gentle wind swept down from Tom's little mountain. It smelled fresh and clean. Tom listened, and he seemed to hear a voice. It said, "I know you won't fail me, my son."

CHAPTER 8

The Swimming Contest

Tom was disappointed when he first saw the College of William and Mary. "The buildings look like rude, misshapen piles," he said to Jupiter.

"You're right," Tom's friend and servant agreed. "Without roofs they would look like brick ovens."

But Tom was greatly impressed with Williamsburg itself. He had never seen such a large town. He and Jupiter rode up and down the unpaved main street. It was called Duke of Gloucester Street. Their horses' hoofs kicked up the powdered oyster shells, which covered the wide street surface like sand. Tom looked at all the shops with great interest. They rode by the Governor's Palace. They visited the Capitol at the end of the street, where the House of Burgesses met.

"Now I'd better report to the college," Tom said, "or they'll be sending out a searching party to find me." Tom met his cousin, Thomas Mann Randolph, as soon as he registered.

Thomas Mann Randolph was delighted to see Tom. He introduced him to other friends. John Page was the one Tom liked best. Later on, Dabney Carr, Tom's best friend, came to college, too.

Tom lived at the college with his friends. He studied very hard, and grew to admire his teacher. William Small was the finest teacher Tom had ever had. He believed that the human mind could solve all of man's troubles.

"Tom," he said, "with study, we could unlock all of nature's secrets. With our knowledge of the past added to the discoveries of the present and the future, we can lead mankind to great things. We can do away with poverty, sickness, and ignorance."

Tom was inspired to study science as he had never done before. He studied sixteen to seventeen hours a day. William Small also encouraged Tom to strengthen his belief in freedom for all. "Resistance to tyranny is obedience to God," he once told his star pupil.

Tom's eyes shone. He would always follow that creed. He was thankful for his good fortune in meeting such an inspiring teacher as Dr. Small. His instructor introduced him to the leading lawyer of Williamsburg. His name was George Wythe.

Wythe was impressed with the tall, young redhead from Albemarle County. "He has a brilliant mind," he told Dr. Small. "We must see that he meets Governor Fauquier (*faw' · kir*)."

"That's a splendid idea," William Small agreed. "Tom plays the violin well. It is very likely that Governor Fauquier will invite him to play in his orchestra."

Tom trembled when he received an invitation to the Governor's Palace. William Small smiled.

"Don't worry. The governor is a perfect gentleman, Tom. You'll be at ease there."

Tom was welcomed by the governor. Each week he went to the palace with William Small and George Wythe. He played second violin in the governor's small orchestra. Tom was much younger than most of the men he met at the palace, but his mind was keen and alert. He listened eagerly as the men discussed topics of the times. He learned a great deal about Europe and the rest of the world. He often went home inspired after a palace visit. He would plunge into his studies with greater vigor. Perhaps some day he might know as much as the governor. Didn't William Small say that the cultivation of the human mind could lead to the greatest heights?

Tom didn't neglect the care of his body during his college days. When he finished studying, he would run about a mile and a half down the Duke of Gloucester Street and back. The town ruffians, who didn't like the college boys, laughed at him.

"Look at the long-legged idiot running like a race horse," one mocked.

"No, he gulps like a fish out of water," another hooted.

Tom just laughed. But his friends were

annoyed. They often got into fights with the town boys. Tom never joined in the fights. He urged his friends not to pay attention to the insults.

"Let's try to become more friendly with them," he advised.

"Never," Thomas Mann Randolph raged. "We'll have nothing to do with them. They call us lace-ruffle dandies. We won't stand for that."

Tom tried to think of a way to stop the fights and bring a better feeling between the two groups. "Next time they insult me," he thought, "I think I know how to call their bluff." And sure enough, the opportunity came the very next day.

While Tom was running along the Duke of Gloucester Street, he was surrounded by a group of young bullies from the town. Tom wasn't frightened when they threatened to rough him up.

"Look, boys," he said. "Why engage in a disgraceful rough and tumble contest? It will get us into trouble with the authorities."

"What shall we do, satin pants, play patty cakes?" smirked the leader of the ruffians.

"No," Tom said. "I challenge any one of you to a swimming race."

"Huh," laughed the leader. "You're too much of a dandy to last even one length of the mill pond."

Tom's anger rose. "Do any of you accept my challenge? We'll make it one of endurance. The one who swims the pond the most times wins."

The leader laughed grimly. "You've got yourself a race," he said. "But don't try to back out of it. We'll expect you at the mill pond tomorrow morning."

"I'll be there," Tom said.

The next morning Tom's friends accompanied him to the mill pond. "It's a quarter of a mile wide," John Page said.

"Shall we follow you in a boat?" Dabney Carr asked.

"No," Tom said, setting his lips firmly. "We must impress these boys that we are not dandies. I won't need a boat."

93

Thomas Mann Randolph started the race off by firing a pistol. "Don't swim too fast, Tom," he warned. "Remember, it's an endurance race."

A mighty cheer went up as Tom and Amos Rolls, the town's best swimmer, plunged into the water. The towners went wild as Amos quickly forged into the lead. But Tom, undisturbed, swam steadily along. He didn't hear the jeers of the towners as Amos opened up a tremendous lead. He just plowed along at his own pace. His years of hunting, running, riding, and swimming in the Rivanna stood him in good stead. His body was in top physical condition. He didn't feel at all tired. After five laps of the mill pond he caught up with and passed Amos. The gasping town boy had to be pulled out of the water after eight laps. He was exhausted and gulped for air.

"Stop, Tom, you've won!" the college boys shrieked. But Tom kept right on swimming.

"I'm going to teach these towners a lesson," he thought. "When I'm done, they'll never

again call us names." He started another lap.

He finished the tenth lap, the eleventh, and the twelfth before he began to get weary. Then he thought of the days when he swam in the Rivanna with his father. It gave him a new strength. "I'll swim one more lap," he muttered. He finished the thirteenth lap with a sprint and walked up on the shore. Even the towners cheered for him.

"You broke the pond record," Amos Rolls gasped. "They say an Indian swam it twelve times. But you even beat his record."

Tom shook the town boy's hand. "Well, Amos," he said with a twinkle in his eye, "I guess that proves we college boys are not satin suit, lace-ruffle dandies."

Amos smiled weakly. "At least one of you is not," he said, as he walked away.

Tom enjoyed his two years at the College of William and Mary. He often saw Shakespeare's plays in Williamsburg. He also went to the Raleigh Tavern, a fine inn, where he danced with the local belles. He learned to dress as nicely and correctly as any of the

Tidewater aristocrats. He also saw George Washington at the House of Burgesses. He was greatly impressed and wrote to his sister Jane about him.

"He's even taller than Father was," he told her in the letter. "He's very strong and solid as an oak. I hope sometime to meet him and to talk with him."

He met the leading architect of Virginia at

George Wythe's house. He was Richard Taliafero, George Wythe's father-in-law.

Tom was fascinated to talk of building and architecture with Mr. Taliafero. In the back of his mind he kept the dream of building a grand house on top of his mountain. Any information he learned about building homes, he eagerly copied down in one of his notebooks.

He went home for short vacations, but he always rushed back to Williamsburg. He wanted to learn all he could about the manners and customs of the people. The more he studied them, the more he thought about becoming a lawyer.

When he was ready to graduate from the College of William and Mary in 1726, he had a long talk with William Small. His teacher was delighted with Tom's plans for further study.

"I'm happy you are going to continue to learn, Tom," he said. "It will make a great man of you."

"I even know in whose office I'd like to study," Tom said.

"I believe I can guess," Dr. Small smiled. "George Wythe?"

"If he'll have me," Tom said.

"I know he will," Dr. Small said. "In fact, we were discussing it the other day. He'll feel honored that you wish to study under him."

Tom graduated from college at the head of his class. Over in England, George III finished his second year as absolute ruler of the British Empire. The selfish, stubborn king would have laughed at Tom's new creed, *Resistance to tyranny is obedience to God.* But the tyrant had never even heard of Thomas Jefferson. He would some day, and have reason to regret it.

CHAPTER 9

Tom's Hardest Case

Tom studied law for five years. He lived in Williamsburg, but he frequently went home to Shadwell to supervise things. In 1765, when Tom was twenty-two years old, Dabney Carr married Tom's sister Martha. Tom was very happy at this joyous occasion. But in October, 1765, Tom received terrible news. His beloved sister, Jane, died suddenly. Tom was heartbroken. His good, kind sister was gone. He went alone to his mountain and brooded there. He remembered how they played and sang together. He remembered how they walked through the woods and gathered flowers. He remembered how she took care of him when he was little. Tears ran down his cheeks. Unashamed, he cried for a long time.

Then he stood up and breathed in deeply. "I'll justify Jane's faith in me," Tom said determinedly. "I'll do the great things Jane and I talked about."

He went to Williamsburg and studied harder than ever. He often met Patrick Henry in the law courts. Patrick had studied law for only six months before being admitted to practice.

George Wythe, who was on the examining board, and another gentleman on the board had been so charmed by Patrick Henry's magic voice that they had signed his license.

Tom often invited Patrick to stay at his room in the boarding house. They played violin duets for many happy hours.

One day Patrick was very excited. "The King has no right to tax us without our having something to say about it. I'm going to speak about it tomorrow in the House of Burgesses."

Tom agreed. "Only our own House of

102

Burgesses should have the power to tax us,"
he said.

The next day the chamber of the House
of Burgesses was crowded. Tom couldn't get
in, but he stayed out in the corridor where he
could at least see and listen.

Patrick Henry's voice was sincere and
strong as he made his speech against the right
of the King to tax without representation.
Thomas Jefferson listened eagerly. He didn't
miss a word. Then a new excitement arose
as Patrick Henry came to the climax of his
speech against the Stamp Act. Some of his lis-
teners thought that he was saying too much
against the King, and they jumped to their
feet in protest.

"Treason, treason!" shouted some of the
older deputies.

Patrick Henry was not afraid. When the
room became quiet, he finished his speech
triumphantly. In a clear, ringing voice he
shouted, "If this be treason, make the most
of it!"

Tom was spellbound. He clapped and

cheered for the great speech. "I can't speak as well as Patrick Henry," he thought. "But someday I'll write against such injustices as the Stamp Act and taxation without representation. I shall use my pen against tyranny. I shall stand for natural laws — the laws of God and nature. I believe that God intended all men to be free."

He spoke his views to George Wythe. The older man was more conservative.

"Be careful to whom you tell these new ideas," he warned, "or you might end up on the gallows alongside Patrick Henry."

Tom shook his head grimly. "Virginians will not stand by to see other Virginians hung," he said. "When that time comes, we'll take up arms to defend ourselves."

George Wythe put his hand on Tom's shoulder. "I envy your fiery youth," he said. "But you'll calm down when you grow older. You'll change."

"I never shall," Tom thought.

When Tom's hard studies were over, he took his bar examination. He passed with ease. He argued cases in the courts of Virginia for seven years. He made a fine lawyer. He didn't appeal to the emotions of the jury the way Patrick Henry did. He appealed to reason. Although his voice wasn't impressive like Patrick's, he studied his facts so carefully and prepared his cases so well, that soon he had more work than he could handle. He argued over one thousand cases in the seven years he practiced.

Tom made about three thousand dollars a year from his law practice. That was a great deal of money in those days. However, he didn't practice law because of the money. He was wealthy from the income of Shadwell and his other inheritances. He practiced to help people.

Sometimes, he made himself unpopular by trying to help people. Once, he tried to help a young Negro, Sam Howell, win his freedom. The judge would not even hear his arguments, and he dismissed the case. But Thomas Jefferson still believed that all men are born free, and ought to remain free.

During the time Tom Jefferson practiced law, he started to build his house on his beloved mountain. He called it Monticello, which means "little mountain" in Italian. He cleared the top of the mountain of trees and leveled it. A small brick building was erected. The underbrush was burned away. Tom supervised everything himself. The plantation workers were taught to make bricks, nails, and other materials. Monticello nails became famous throughout Virginia.

In February, 1770, Shadwell burned to the ground. The family moved to an overseer's house, but Tom moved into the unfinished brick cottage on top of the mountain. While there, he studied the work of the great Italian architect, Andrea Palladio. From him, he got the idea of building his main house in Roman style. For many hours a day he designed his dream mansion. The plans included stately columns like those of the ancient Roman temples.

Tom was happy as Monticello began to take form. The one thing he needed now was a good wife. He met a beautiful woman, Martha Wayles Skelton. She lived at her father's home, which was called The Forest. She played the harpsichord, and Tom played the violin. One happy day she consented to become his wife. When the wedding ceremony was over, they set out in a small carriage on the hundred-mile trip to Monticello. On the way a snowstorm developed.

"Shall we stop at an inn?" Tom asked.

"No," Martha Wayles Jefferson said. "Let's drive on."

The blizzard grew worse. When they reached the estate of Blenheim, eight miles from Monticello, the carriage could go no further on the snow-blocked roads.

"Let's stay here for tonight," Tom urged.

"Nonsense," his wife answered. "I must reach my new home as soon as possible. I can't wait to see it."

They mounted fresh horses and rode off into the night. Finally, they reached Monticello. The cottage was dark. All the servants had gone to bed. The newlyweds didn't awaken them. They opened the door and went in.

"Welcome to Monticello," Tom cried, as he lighted the wood in the fireplace.

"What a lovely cottage," his bride gasped. "Let's call it the honeymoon cottage." And that has been its name for almost two hundred years.

The next year was a happy one for the newlyweds. Their musical duets filled the honeymoon cottage with laughter and music. Monticello began to grow into a wonderful new home. When Tom's daughter, Martha, was born, he was the happiest man in the colony.

He had been elected a member of the House of Burgesses. He had helped the planters of Albemarle County clear the Rivanna of rocks so that now the hogsheads of tobacco could be floated by canoes all the way to the market.

Then another tragedy struck. Dabney Carr died. He was buried in the churchyard at Charlottesville. Tom, who had been away from home, rushed back to Monticello. He comforted his sister, Martha Jefferson Carr, and her five children.

"Martha, you will live with me," he said. "I will be like a father to your children." He always treated the Carr youngsters as his own. Young Peter Carr was like a real son to Tom.

Dabney was not yet thirty years old when he died. He had become a promising lawyer.

Many considered him Patrick Henry's only rival as a great speaker.

Tom had the body of Dabney Carr transferred to a grave on his mountain. He kept the promise he had made to Dabney many years before. He often visited the grave of his friend.

Then the years seemed to vanish. They were boys again, sitting in the branches of the oak tree and dreaming dreams. "I shall not forget those wonderful years, Dabney," he said. "Some day, when my work on earth is done, I shall be buried here alongside you. Then we'll still be as close as we were in life!"

Monticello As It Looks Today

CHAPTER 10

Clouds of War

After Dabney's death Thomas Jefferson would have preferred to spend all of his time at Monticello. He wanted to look after every detail of building his new home. He had such wonderful plans.

"I'm going to build a bed in our room that will lift into the ceiling when we're not using it," he told his wife. "I'm also going to build a special clock. I'm going to use cannon balls for the weights that make the clock go. And I'll fix it so that one of the clock weights will show the day of the week as it unwinds day by day. I'm also going to build an indoor weather vane so we can tell which way the wind is blowing without going outside."

"These plans are wonderful," agreed his wife, "but you will not have time for them now. The colonies need your help in their fight against King George."

Jefferson nodded his head sadly. "I know that, Martha. But whenever I get a chance, I'll come back to you and Monticello."

As a member of the House of Burgesses, Jefferson did outstanding work in those troublesome days. The people of Boston dumped a shipload of tea into the harbor rather than pay the King's tax. King George punished Boston by closing its port. Jefferson led the Virginia House of Burgesses to declare a day of prayer and fasting in sympathy with their brothers in Massachusetts. Governor Dunmore had been sent by the King to rule Virginia with an iron hand. He called an end to the meeting of the House of Burgesses. Nevertheless, the burgesses met in the Raleigh Tavern.

Some of the gentlemen suggested that men representing all the colonies get together to discuss their common problems. It was agreed that it would be a grand idea. Jefferson wrote a paper to guide the members from Virginia. Some of the older Virginians thought that Jefferson's guide was worded too strongly. But others liked it so much that it was printed as a pamphlet. It was read widely in the colonies and also in England. Thomas Jefferson became known as a leader in the fight for liberty.

He pointed out many injustices in his paper. He said that the King had no right to suspend the legislature of New York; the King had no right to tax without the people having something to say about it, and that the God who gave us life gave us liberty at the same time.

A brave new spirit was sweeping through the thirteen colonies.

Later on, the Virginians called another meeting in Richmond, because relations with England were getting worse instead of better. They met in the church now known as St. John's Church. Again Patrick Henry arose. He was annoyed because many con-

115

servative Virginians were still loyal to the King.

Jefferson listened in thrilled attention as Patrick Henry cried, ". . . peace, peace — but there is no peace. . . . Why stand we here idle? Is life so dear, or peace so sweet, as to be purchased at the price of chains and slavery? Forbid it, Almighty God! I know not what course others may take; but as for me, give me liberty, or give me death!"

Even Jefferson was shaken as Patrick Henry sat down. It was a call for arming for defense. It was a step toward war.

By a close vote of 65 to 60, the delegates voted to arm the colony. Some of the older men were afraid to take such a drastic step. But the young leaders like Thomas Jefferson, Patrick Henry, and George Washington won the day.

There was to be a meeting in Philadelphia of men from all over the colonies. Jefferson was one of the men selected to go from Virginia. Before he could go, the governor, Lord Dunmore, became afraid of the new war-like spirit in Virginia. He had the gun-powder transferred from Williamsburg to a British warship. Patrick Henry led an armed band of men to get the ammunition back. The governor refused to give it to them. However, the colonists forced him to pay for the powder.

Very soon after that, Jefferson went to Philadelphia with Richard, one of his servants. He was welcomed at the meeting because his writings had made him well-known. This meeting became known as the First Continental Congress. Although he was the second youngest man here, Jefferson was given important committee work by the leaders, John Adams, Ben Franklin, and others. On June 15, 1775, the Congress elected George Washington Commander-in-Chief of the colonial forces. Jefferson stood and cheered with the others when General Washington and some picked troops marched through the streets on their way to Boston.

"Our hopes and dreams lie in the hands of that strong man," he thought. "George Wash-

ington is the leader who can bring us victory."

The news of the battle of Bunker Hill swept through Philadelphia. War had finally come. In August, Jefferson finished his duties and went home to Monticello. He became busy building his home. He had a gardener from Italy who helped him lay out the vineyards. He planted new apple, cherry, and apricot trees. He enjoyed the short vacation, and he even had time to play musical duets with his wife.

Then more sadness struck him. Their new baby, Jane, died. His wife became ill, and Jefferson worried about her health. His own health was not good either. He developed terrific headaches. But his duty to his country called. He returned to Congress where he stayed until December.

In the North George Washington was fighting the British around Boston. The colonists in Virginia were now in open rebellion. They instructed the Virginia delegates to Congress to propose that the colonies should be free of England. The colonists wanted Congress to write a declaration of independence and to make plans for a new government.

Jefferson's mother died that spring, and he had a new grief. His gentle, kind mother, who had taught him so much, was gone. He mourned a long time for her. His own health became poor. His headaches became worse. However, when the call came to go to Philadelphia in May, he answered it.

"Just as my father before me," he said. "I cannot ignore my duty."

His wife agreed. "Go, Tom," she said. "Your country needs you as never before."

In Philadelphia he went to see Ben Randolph, a cabinetmaker. He had stayed at the Randolph home the last time he had been in Philadelphia.

"Ben," said Tom, "here are the plans for a folding writing desk. Can you make such a desk?"

Ben looked at the drawings. "They are simple to follow. I'll have it finished for you very soon."

"I'm living in the home of Graff, the bricklayer," Jefferson said. "I would like you to bring the desk there when it's finished."

In a few days Ben Randolph brought Jefferson the small folding desk.

"Thank you," Jefferson smiled. "It may be that I shall write some important papers on this desk."

Thomas Jefferson worked hard on various committees. But he took time out to write out a new constitution for Virginia. George Wythe took it back with him to Williamsburg. On the seventh of June, 1776, Richard Henry Lee presented to Congress the proposal that the Virginia assembly had adopted. It was a call for freedom. Jefferson listened attentively to the bold words. Many of them were his words, his thoughts, his dreams.

"These United Colonies are, and of right ought to be, free and independent states," Richard Henry Lee stated. "They are absolved from all allegiance to the British crown."

Bedlam arose. Some of the delegates from the middle states and South Carolina weren't ready yet to take such a frightening step. This was treason and could be punished by hanging. It was decided to delay action until July first, and to appoint a committee to draft a declaration of independence.

Thomas Jefferson of Virginia, John Adams of Massachusetts, Benjamin Franklin of Pennsylvania, Roger Sherman of Connecticut, and Robert Livingston of New York were appointed to be on the committee.

The committee met in Franklin's house on Bristol Street. Franklin was ill at the time, but his mind was as keen as ever. "Five people are too many to write the declaration," he said. "Let's choose one person to compose it."

"I nominate Thomas Jefferson," John Adams said.

"I haven't enough experience," Jefferson said.

"Nonsense," Franklin declared. "I've read your writings. You're the man for the job."

"Besides," John Adams added, "it's better for a Virginian to do this job. We in Massachusetts are getting the bad name of radicals and troublemakers." He shook Jefferson's hand. "And if that's not enough, Tom Jefferson, you're easily the best writer here."

Jefferson flushed under the praise. Then he stood up. He was the tallest man in the room. He ran his fingers through his red hair. He wasn't handsome, but his hazel eyes flashed as he smiled. "I'll do my best, gentlemen. Good day."

He went back to his room. He took out his new writing desk. He sharpened his pens and gathered many sheets of paper. "Mrs. Graff," he called out, "see that I am not disturbed. I have some important work to do."

CHAPTER 11

The Declaration of Independence

All through the hot month of June, 1776, Thomas Jefferson labored on the Declaration of Independence. His little room was stifling. Green-winged horseflies from a nearby stable annoyed him terribly. But he worked grimly on. This was the moment he had prepared for, all his thirty-three years. For this great moment he had studied law, government, and politics. For this he had studied about ancient Greece and Rome. This was to be all his hopes and dreams on paper. He often wished he could leave hot, unbearable Philadelphia. He wanted to write the declaration on his cool little mountain. Of course he couldn't do it, so he did the next best thing. In his imagination he made his beloved mountain come to him. He thought of the old days when he was young. He thought of his father, his mother, his sister Jane, and Dabney Carr. Although they were gone now, their spirits were still with him.

"I am not alone," Jefferson thought. "All my loved ones are with me. They are helping me write this paper." The words he wrote were inspired. "We hold these truths to be self evident, that all men are created equal, that they are endowed by their Creator with certain unalienable rights. Among these are life, liberty, and the pursuit of happiness." Many men may have felt this way before, but none were able to write it down the way Jefferson did.

He wrote further that governments got their power from the consent of the governed, and when the heads of government proved wicked, the people have the right to remove them. Jefferson was a trained lawyer. He wrote down the American people's case against the King in flawless language. The facts were plain for the entire world to see.

Jefferson wrote on angrily that George III had tried to enslave the colonies. He had taxed without representation. He had robbed the seas, burned American towns, and destroyed the lives of the people. He had encouraged the Indians to attack settlers. George III, Jefferson concluded, was a tyrant who was unfit to be a ruler.

Jefferson also wrote against slavery. He denounced it as a cruel, inhuman practice which ought to be abolished. As the hot weeks rolled by, John Adams and Benjamin Franklin sometimes made small suggestions. But it was Jefferson who was the heart and soul of the Declaration of Independence. Patrick Henry may have been the voice of the Revolution, George Washington the sword, but Thomas Jefferson was the mighty pen of the Revolution.

He sat up many weary hours writing and rewriting his paper. He grew pale and sickly.

"Mr. Jefferson, you should rest a little from your long hours of work," urged his landlady.

"No, I must not stop," he said. "In this document are the hopes and dreams of generations to come."

Never before in the world's history had a man declared that God guaranteed all men life, liberty, and the pursuit of happiness. Up to now men had argued that only kings had a divine right to rule, that God had willed them to be over the common man. Jefferson flung this lie into their teeth. "No!" he thundered. "A man has a natural right to be free." He knew this declaration was not for America alone. The whole world had to accept it and help the weak thirteen colonies defy mighty Britain.

Jefferson wrote so stirringly that help did come. It came mostly from France. But other countries also approved of the new ideas in human liberty.

Finally on June twenty-eighth it was finished. The committee presented the declara-

tion to Congress. On July first, the debate
started. For three frightfully hot days, Jefferson squirmed and suffered as Congress went
over every word he had written. To his dis-
may they struck out every line against
slavery. Georgia and South Carolina were
mainly against eliminating slavery. But many
northerners were also guilty. They didn't
want slavery abolished. They carried the
slaves in their ships. They made enormous
profits in this inhuman practice.

Jefferson felt sick. "Some day," he muttered to Franklin, "our country will suffer
many evils because slavery was not abolished
at this time."

Old gray-haired Benjamin Franklin nodded.
"I know that, my boy, but cheer up. Congress
is keeping almost everything else you wrote.
I'm proud of you."

On July 4, 1776, the Declaration of Independence was accepted. A great spirit of joy
surged through the colonies. The Liberty
Bell was rung in Independence Square in
Philadelphia. Copies of the Declaration were

read to cheering thousands throughout the country. George Washington had it read to his troops on Long Island. On Monday, Esek Hopkins of the new American Navy read the Declaration in Independence Square. The enormous crowd cheered time after time as the immortal phrases boomed out, "All men are created equal; all men are entitled to life,

liberty, and the pursuit of happiness."

When Commander Hopkins read the concluding portion, a mighty yell went up. "And for the support of this Declaration . . . we mutually pledge to each other our lives, our fortunes, and our sacred honor."

"Three cheers for the Declaration of Independence," the people shouted. They

rushed to the state house and tore down the royal coat of arms. They built a huge bonfire and burned this symbol of tyranny.

Jefferson, weak and exhausted from his task, was satisfied. He had created a new path of liberty for mankind to follow. It took almost a month before the Declaration was formally signed. John Hancock signed first, in big, bold letters.

"Now King George can read it without specs," he chuckled.

"We have done it," someone said. "We have declared ourselves free. Now we must hang together."

Franklin's eyes twinkled. "Or we shall all hang separately," he added.

Jefferson said nothing. He had written the Declaration, but now he must try to make it work. He wanted to do a great deal more building on Monticello. He wanted to be with his family. But he had his duty to do. "Writing is one thing," he thought. "But if I don't bring these ideas into practice, it will be useless. I'll go back to Virginia, and for the first time in history, I shall attempt to put these ideas of human liberty into written laws. These laws will guarantee forever what I have written in the Declaration of Independence."

CHAPTER 12

Laws for Liberty

After he wrote the Declaration of Independence, Jefferson went back to Virginia where he served as a member of the legislature. His wife was delighted to have her husband home at Monticello.

"Your hard work is over now, Tom," she said. "You need a rest. Writing the Declaration of Independence was a tremendous task."

Jefferson smiled. "The hard work is still ahead. Now I must give true meaning to the words I wrote. Laws must be passed to guarantee the thoughts and purposes of the Declaration of Independence so no tyrant can try to enslave the people again."

"You will meet much opposition," Martha Jefferson said.

"I know it," Jefferson sighed. "But freedom and human liberty have never come easily. I am willing to pay the price to protect it."

First, he had a law passed to change an old land law which said that a great estate could never be broken up into smaller estates or farms. Jefferson knew that this land law was bad because it meant that the large land owners would become a special class with wealth, power, and privileges. "We're fighting a war now to do away with special titles and privileges," he said.

Jefferson also drew up a bill to change another land law which said that the eldest son in the family inherits the entire estate when his father dies. The younger children could not be left any of the land. This could lead to the same evils as the other land law. But the aristocratic class in Virginia, who were large land owners and wanted to keep things that way, fought Jefferson tooth and

136

nail. Not until many years later was the old law changed. Jefferson was not even in Virginia at that time. His duty to his country took him to other important posts. But his faithful follower, James Madison, carried on the fight to final victory.

The reform Jefferson was most proud of was his bill on religious freedom. He proposed that all men could worship God as they pleased. The state church of Virginia was the Church of England. All Virginians were expected to support that church.

The battle over religious freedom lasted more than ten years. Once more Madison carried on the fight. Jefferson was in Paris, London, and Washington serving his country at that time. Eventually, the bill was passed. It became the policy of our country which we all enjoy. A man can worship God as he pleases anywhere in the United States. We should be thankful to Thomas Jefferson and James Madison for this precious liberty which we take for granted.

Jefferson did not win all his battles for

human liberty. He tried to do away with slavery, but failed. He tried to put in a system of free education for all. He wanted to have primary, or "hundred" schools as he called them, established. After three years in these schools, the best students were to go to grammar schools built and supported by the state. The students were to live at the grammar schools. Those whose parents could afford it would pay. The others would attend free of charge. From these schools called the "tens," the best students would go on to the College of William and Mary. Again, those who couldn't pay would attend free.

His enemies sneered at him. "The common people are trash," they cried. "We must educate only the sons of the aristocratic classes."

"No!" Jefferson cried. "I believe in the aristocracy of talent and virtue. This belongs to all classes."

In spite of Jefferson's efforts, Congress would not vote for public education. However, years later our country did adopt his ideas. To this day we have the blessings of

His enemies sneered at him.

free public education, thanks to such men as Thomas Jefferson. Jefferson never ceased to fight for the education of the common man.

When he was Ambassador to France, he wrote to his former teacher, George Wythe. "Preach, my dear sir, a crusade against ignorance. Establish and improve the law for educating the common people." He went on to say that education would safeguard freedom and assure honest government.

Thomas Jefferson also served on a committee to rewrite the laws of Virginia. They were extremely strict. Many petty, minor crimes were punishable by death.

Jefferson rewrote most of the laws. He stated that only treason and murder deserved the death sentence. He made the laws more humane and kind. "Let us reform our criminals," he said, "not just punish them."

He first worked out the idea that men should be used for work while in jail, rather than be left to rot in cells and dungeons. Again his enemies fought him hard and long. And again James Madison had to complete the final and lasting victory many years later.

Jefferson also tried to establish a free state library at Richmond. This, too, was defeated. In time, however, free libraries were adopted throughout our entire country.

Jefferson's battle to free the minds, bodies, and souls of men firmly established democracy in our young country. Even the battles he lost helped to lay the foundation for future good laws. Without the work of Thomas Jefferson and James Madison, our country might have developed into a tyrant state instead of into a wonderful democracy.

CHAPTER 13

Wartime Governor

Thomas Jefferson served for ten years in the Virginia legislature. They were happy years. Whether he won or lost his battles, he knew he was helping the cause of the common man. In June, 1779, he was elected governor of Virginia. He felt strange as he entered the palace at Williamsburg and took up his quarters. Many years before, he had visited there as a guest of Governor Fauquier. Now he, Thomas Jefferson, was governor.

The Jefferson family joined him, and he got down to the serious business of leading wartime Virginia. Jefferson had a council of eight men elected by the legislature to guide

143

him. There were many difficult problems. The British blockade of ports prevented any trade with foreign countries. Paper money had little or no value because there was so much of it. To make matters worse, the crops failed. Many people and even the farm animals were starving. Salt was lacking and impossible to obtain. Because of this, many of the meat supplies rotted and could not be eaten. Tom's friends urged him to become a dictator until the situation got better.

"Do as you see fit," they advised. "Ignore the advice of the legislature. This is an emergency. There is no time for discussion."

Jefferson shook his head. "No. I am determined that the outcome of this war shall not be the loss of the freedom the army is fighting for. I am duty bound to carry out the will of the assembly."

Whenever General Washington wanted more men, arms, and supplies from Virginia, Jefferson saw that he got them. Many people objected to sending the best troops of Virginia out of the state.

"Why should we send our soldiers away?" they asked. "We'll be helpless if the enemy attacks us here."

"We must think of the good of the entire thirteen states," Jefferson said. "General Washington knows best where the troops are needed most."

Then Virginia received a terrible shock. Some of the state's finest soldiers under General Washington were captured at Charleston, South Carolina. Jefferson's enemies attacked him with great strength.

"Don't send any more men to help General Washington," they said. "We sacrificed some of our best troops in vain."

Jefferson was grieved, but he did not listen. "I still will help our Commander-in-Chief," he said.

In the spring, the capitol was moved from Williamsburg to Richmond. At the end of the year, Jefferson was again elected governor. He appointed James Monroe commissioner of information and assigned him to the Carolina area. "Now," Jefferson said, "my reports will be correct. James Monroe is smart. He'll do a good job of reporting what the enemy is up to."

Thomas Jefferson continued to send new troops, wagons, and tents to the South Carolina battlefields. All were lost in a terrible defeat at Camden. Many Virginians became discouraged. Some deserted from the militia. Others, especially in the southern counties, swore allegiance to the King again. But Jefferson never gave up. He issued more calls for men, arms, and supplies.

Virginia was most open to attacks from the sea. It had a long coast line and many broad rivers which led into the interior of the state.

General Washington sent General von Steuben to help Jefferson defend Virginia. Von Steuben was a Prussian. He did not believe in strict enforcement of law during wartime. He asked Jefferson for free white labor and for Negroes to help build a fort below Richmond.

Jefferson refused. "The law does not give me the power to draft a man to labor even

146

for the public good without his consent."

Von Steuben's face grew red with anger. "Then give me the Negroes," he howled.

"I cannot do that," Jefferson answered, "not without their masters' consent."

"I will send my troops to get all the horses in the neighborhood," Von Steuben said. "The army can use all the horses we can get."

Jefferson shook his head. "The farmers are starving," he explained. "They need the horses for work in the fields."

General von Steuben was disgusted. "I must insist that you give me twenty thousand men to send to General Greene," he demanded.

This time Jefferson was even more firm. "I cannot weaken the state any further," he said.

Von Steuben remained angry. He wrote a letter to General Washington. "This man thinks more of law and the rights of the common man than he does of anything else," he complained.

The traitor, Benedict Arnold, led several raids against Virginia. General Lafayette was sent by Washington to defend Virginia. The brilliant young Frenchman saved Richmond, the wartime capital of the state. Jefferson thought Benedict Arnold would not return.

He sent more troops to help General Greene in South Carolina. But the traitor did return with many more ships and men. This time he succeeded in burning Richmond. He destroyed valuable military stores and important government records.

A storm of protest against Jefferson arose from his enemies. "Why doesn't the governor do something?" they howled.

"He's doing a poor job," others said. "He was two days late in getting the militia ready."

Jefferson was heartbroken, but he took the blame himself. "I did not realize the full strength of the British forces," he said. "I was not informed of the seriousness of the raid."

To add to Jefferson's troubles, his youngest daughter, Lucy, died. Jefferson didn't have a chance to grieve. Benedict Arnold and the British fleet attacked once more. This time Lafayette managed to save Richmond. But the traitor burned valuable tobacco stores in Manchester and Petersburg. Then the worst possible disaster came to Virginia. General Cornwallis and the main British

149

army invaded the state. They joined forces with Benedict Arnold at Petersburg.

Jefferson had to move the capital to Charlottesville, in the central part of the state. His frightened council did not follow him there. Only two members of the eight ever arrived. Only forty members of the legislature made the trip to Charlottesville.

Jefferson did his best to cheer up his people. "The English cannot hold out," he said, "for all the world is against them."

A group of Illinois Indians visited him at the new capital. Jefferson smoked the peace pipe and gave them an encouraging talk.

"My brothers," he said, "after six years of war, our enemy has gained no more ground than room to bury the slain warriors."

The Indians were impressed and remained loyal to the Americans.

Generals Cornwallis and Benedict Arnold had over seven thousand trained men in Virginia. Lafayette had less than half that number. The American troops had little training. Yet the British could not destroy the

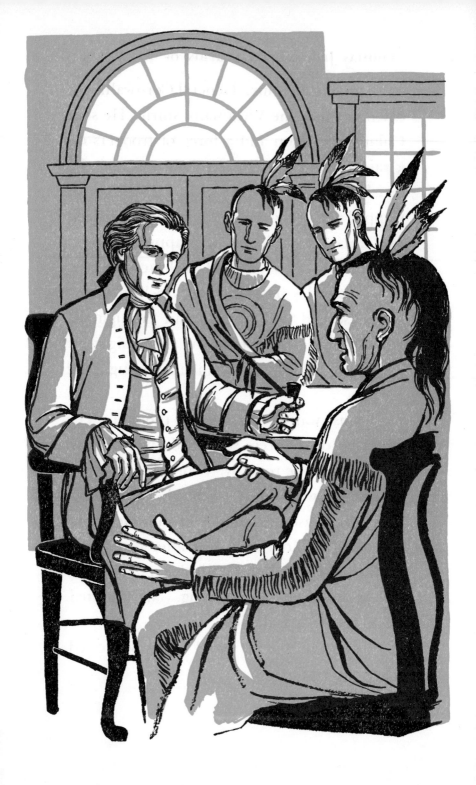

small American army. General Cornwallis decided to break the Virginians' spirit. He sent Colonel Tarleton and a force of troopers on a raid to capture Thomas Jefferson and the legislature at Charlottesville. The British stopped at Cuckoo Inn to rest. They were seen by Captain Jack Jouett, a strapping six-foot-four American soldier. Charlottesville was forty-five miles from the inn. Jack mounted his horse and took a back trail through the woods. The British took the main highway. Jack rode like a madman all through the night.

"I must warn Jefferson," he thought. The branches of the trees scratched and whipped at his face as he rode by. Soon the blood was running down Jack's face, but he didn't stop. Faster and faster he urged his tired horse on. He reached Monticello just after dawn. He awakened Jefferson from his sleep.

"The British are coming," he shouted. "You must leave at once."

"They won't come here!" Jefferson cried. "Not way out here."

"They're coming," Jack Jouett insisted. "You and your family must escape."

Jefferson immediately issued orders. First, he told Jack to warn the legislators. "Tell them to go to Staunton. That's forty miles west of here. They'll be safe there."

Jack leaped on his horse and rode the three miles to Charlottesville.

Jefferson turned to Jupiter. "Drive Mrs. Jefferson and the children to Colonel Cole's house. I'll join them there later."

"Please come with us, Tom," his wife begged as the carriage prepared to leave.

"No," he said. "I must burn the important state papers. Nothing of importance must fall into the hands of the enemy."

The carriage rolled off. Jefferson burned the secret papers. Martin and another slave, Caesar, began hiding the silverware under the porch. Jefferson, armed with his short sword and a telescope, hurriedly left Monticello. He started up nearby Carter's Mountain. At a lookout point he stopped and trained his telescope towards Charlottesville.

No British troopers were anywhere in sight.
Tom felt foolish. "They're not coming. I can
still go back to Monticello," he thought. He
started down, but soon he noticed he had lost
his short sword. He went back to pick it up.
Again he trained his telescope on the town.
This time he was shocked to see the whole
area overrun with redcoats. Many troopers
were already climbing the slopes of Monti-

cello. Tom quickly rushed through the woods and joined his family who were resting at Colonel Cole's residence.

In the meantime, Captain McLeod, in charge of the British soldiers, burst into Monticello. Martin was so surprised that he dropped the plank on the porch under which the silver was hidden. Poor Caesar was locked down there in the darkness with the silverware.

The British stayed three days, and all that time Caesar was trapped under the porch. He was so loyal to Mr. Jefferson that he never made a sound. He knew the British would steal the silverware if they found it. Martin

was also loyal. The British threatened him with death unless he told them where Mr. Jefferson and his family had hidden. Martin refused to tell. Finally, the British had to leave without their prize, the governor of Virginia.

While the legislature was meeting in Staunton, Jefferson's term of office ended. The legislature elected Thomas Nelson as the new governor. Some of Jefferson's enemies, angered because the British seemed to be winning the war, made the following resolution: *"Resolved,* That the conduct of the executive of this state for the past twelve months be investigated."

Jefferson was heartbroken when he heard the news. After all he had suffered as wartime governor, this was to be his reward — the disapproval of fellow Virginians. Then some good news thrilled all Virginia. General Washington and the French fleet trapped Cornwallis at Yorktown. Cornwallis surrendered, and the war was over. Had Jefferson been governor one month longer, he could have been a hero, the victorious wartime governor. The legislature wanted to drop the investigation of Jefferson. He wouldn't hear of it. He ran for office as a legislator, and he won. He went in person before the legislature and asked that the charges against him be read. Answering each one, he defended his conduct. As it became evident that he was an honorable man, the legislature rose and cheered him. Thomas Jefferson then resigned.

"I will now retire to private life," he said. "I have given enough to my country."

But the United States needed Jefferson too much. He was soon called back to serve once more. There were many, many hard battles for freedom yet to be won. The War of Independence was won, but the war to free men's minds and bodies was just beginning.

CHAPTER 14

In the Service of His Country

A short time after Jefferson re-signed from the legislature, he had an accident. He fell off his horse, Caractarius, and broke his right arm. Unable to write with his right hand, he learned to write with his left.

He started work on an important project. A Frenchman, called Marbois (*mar · bwah*), was seeking information about America. He drew up a series of questions which he wanted answered. Marbois had been told that Thomas Jefferson was the best-informed man in America. Thomas Jefferson's answers to the Frenchman's questions became a famous book called *Notes on Virginia*.

159

A French scientist by the name of Buffon had stated that all animal life in the New World was small and poor as compared to European animal life.

Jefferson became very angry. "I'll show him that American animal life is as big or bigger than anything in Europe." Jefferson promptly searched out everyone he could for information on the weights of American animals. He proved Buffon wrong. The American animals were not small and poor at all. In many cases they were larger and heavier than European animals. The American world had nothing to be ashamed of in regard to its animal, plant, or human life.

Thomas Jefferson wrote about the grandeur of Virginia and the land to the west. He described the rivers, lakes, mountains, the people, and legends. He wrote so thrillingly of the country he loved that later on the book was widely read. It was read all over Europe and America. The learned men of the Old World were amazed at Jefferson's genius. This American was a fine student of natural history, philosophy, and science. He was as cultured and learned as any aristocrat in Europe.

Then another terrible tragedy, perhaps the worst of all, struck Jefferson. His beloved wife's health began to fail. Jefferson was frantic. But there was nothing the doctors could do. Mrs. Jefferson died soon after the newest baby was born. Jefferson seemed dazed for many weeks. He was finally roused out of his condition by his daughter Patsy.

"Come, Father," she said, one beautiful day. "Let's go for a ride. It will make you feel better."

Jefferson had to be lifted to his horse by Jupiter. He was so weak from his grief that he could hardly sit in his saddle. Every day he and Patsy went for a ride.

Soon he recovered his strength, and Congress asked him to go to Paris to work on a peace treaty. His companions were to be Benjamin Franklin and John Adams. Jefferson and his daughter Patsy left for Philadelphia to await a ship. But the peace treaty was signed before they could get there. Jefferson was disappointed. He had wanted to go to Europe to serve his country and forget about his troubles. He was elected to Congress as a Virginia representative. He did not wish to serve, but he was convinced by James Madison and James Monroe that it was his duty.

While in Congress, he helped introduce some very important bills. He drew up the Ordinance of 1784. This stated that the new states of the Northwest Territory were to be admitted to the United States as equals with the original thirteen states. It meant that all states now and in the future would have equal rights.

"We didn't fight a war for freedom," Jefferson said, "to set up a new tyranny in America." He wanted all slavery to be illegal in the new territory after 1800. This section was voted down. If his idea had been carried out there wouldn't have been enough slave states to carry on the Civil War sixty years later.

Another important bill Jefferson worked

on was the Coinage Bill. "Arithmetic troubles most people," he said to Robert Morris, who presented a complicated plan. "Let's choose something simple."

Dollars became the unit, and the other coins we know such as dimes, pennies, nickels, and quarters were adopted. If it were not for Jefferson we might still be using pounds, shillings, and pence.

Unfortunately Congress didn't accept Jefferson's simple plan for a system of weights and measures.

On May 7, 1784, Congress appointed Jefferson Minister to France. He was to help Benjamin Franklin and John Adams make trade agreements for the United States. Jefferson was delighted to go. He was disgusted with the Congress.

"Whether Congress met at Philadelphia, Princeton, or Annapolis," he wrote, "many representatives did not show up. Those who did argued violently over petty details for days and months." Jefferson was glad to be rid of the endless arguments.

"Patsy," he said, "you will go with me to Paris. I will put you in a good school there. Polly and little Lucy can stay with Aunt Eppes."

Patsy was overjoyed. "I'll be glad to go," she cried. "It should be great fun."

"And much hard work," her father replied. "I am only a farmer. Now I will have to do a merchant's work." But Jefferson did splendidly in France. He helped Franklin and Adams draw up treaties.

He was also interested in everything about Europe. He traveled all over Europe and took notes. He sent home many samples of new fruits, vegetables, and trees. He copied Europe's buildings and architecture. He talked to its leading citizens. He met Lafayette again. He watched the growing French Revolution.

Tom Jefferson became Ambassador to France when Franklin resigned.

"No one can replace Benjamin Franklin," he said. "I merely follow him."

The French liked Thomas Jefferson. They

respected him. But when he traveled to London, he received a poor welcome. The King of England turned his back on Jefferson. The writer of the Declaration of Independence was amazed.

"I should expect the King at least to have good manners," he said.

Jefferson went back to France. While visiting a farmer, he sketched a new idea for a plow. He sent it to the United States. It turned out to be a good one. Jefferson was happy. His keen mind was always searching for new ways to help his country and all mankind. After five years he was recalled to the United States.

"Now I can retire to Monticello," he thought. But George Washington felt otherwise. He chose Jefferson for his Secretary of State. Jefferson came into contact with Alexander Hamilton, the Secretary of the Treasury. The two men became bitter rivals. Hamilton believed in the rule of the few. Jefferson believed that education should be free to the sons of all men.

"The common mob is not to be trusted," Hamilton thundered. "It will make errors."

Jefferson answered, "Error of opinion may be tolerated when reason is left free to combat it."

Washington was upset by the strife between his two advisors, but he needed both of them. Jefferson wanted to resign to keep the peace, but Washington wouldn't let him. Jefferson became more and more attached to the rights of the common man; Hamilton grew more and more devoted to the privilege of the few. The two men formed the first political parties in the United States. Jefferson's followers were called Republicans. Hamilton's were called Federalists. Later on, Jefferson's party grew into the present-day Democratic party.

At this time the capital of the United States was New York City. Many sections of the country were dissatisfied with this arrangement. Jefferson worked out a compromise with Hamilton whereby Washington, D.C., became the capital of the United States. It would take ten years to build a new city. Washington hired the Frenchman, L'Enfant (*lahn · fahn'*), as the architect. Jefferson worked closely with him and planned many of the public buildings.

While Jefferson was in France, he had encouraged James Madison to add the Bill of Rights to the Constitution. "Human liberty must never be left to chance," he wrote. "It must be written in black and white as laws to protect freedom; then it can never be taken away." He was always watchful to defend liberty. The attacks on him by the aristocratic class became more bitter. Finally, George Washington let Jefferson resign as Secretary of State.

"Now," Jefferson thought, "I can surely go back to Monticello and do the things I have always wanted to do." But it was not to be.

After George Washington's second term, Thomas Jefferson was nominated as the presidential candidate by the Republican party. He ran second to John Adams, the Federalist candidate. According to the law of those days, Jefferson now became vice-president. The man who received the second number of votes became vice-president even though he was of another party.

Jefferson served as vice-president and again he fought for the rights of the common people. As head of the Senate he could not vote unless there was a tie, but he had great influence. Many bills were passed or defeated according to what Thomas Jefferson decided.

After John Adams served one term, Jefferson knew he had to run for President. The Federalists had passed two bills which endangered liberty. These bills permitted the government to jail many people for speaking against the government.

Jefferson was furious. "We fought for the right to speak against the King," he cried. "This is tyranny of the same sort. But this time we will fight with votes, not bullets. We can have a revolution without bloodshed."

His followers agreed. "You must lead us in this fight," they cried.

"I will," he said. "I have sworn upon the

altar of God eternal hostility against every form of tyranny over the mind of man."

The Republicans chose Thomas Jefferson and Aaron Burr as their candidates. The Federalist candidates were Adams and Pinckney. Some people were surprised when Jefferson and Burr received the largest number of votes, but neither could become President, because they were tied. Congress had to break the deadlock. They voted many times, but neither candidate received the majority of nine states. It was bitterly cold in Washington, and snow covered the ground. Time after time, the legislature had to climb the stairs to the Capitol and vote, but the deadlock still could not be broken. Finally, Hamilton, who respected Jefferson even though he opposed him, swung his followers to Jefferson.

"I distrust Aaron Burr," he said. "I know Jefferson is an honest man."

John Adams also swung his followers to Jefferson. On the thirty-sixth ballot Thomas Jefferson was elected President of the United

States. The boy who had traveled from Shadwell to Tuckahoe on the back of a horse at the age of two had come a long way.

CHAPTER 15

President of
the United States

Thomas Jefferson officially became President in Washington, D.C., on March 4, 1801. The streets were muddy and unpaved. Stumps of trees jutted from the ground. The boardinghouses were overcrowded and uncomfortable, yet the people were happy. Thomas Jefferson, the friend of the common man, was President.

The Federalists, however, were not happy. "Thomas Jefferson will ruin the country with his insane ideas," they said. "The mob isn't fit to rule."

But Thomas Jefferson didn't listen to his opponents. "I believe our Republican gov-

173

ernment will some day be the strongest on earth," he said.

The first thing he did was to free the people who had been put in jail for talking against the government. Congress repealed the acts which had caused them to be jailed.

"Free men must have the right to criticize their government," Jefferson proclaimed.

He appointed James Madison as Secretary of State. He reduced the public debt and lessened the cost of government. Unlike Hamilton, Jefferson told the people about the government finances. The country prospered. Jefferson brought good times to the United States. One thing, however, annoyed his friends. The President refused to fire the men John Adams had put in office before he left Washington.

"I will never remove a man just because of his political beliefs," he said. "If a man is unfit, I'll replace him. If he is doing his job, I don't care if he's a Federalist or a Republican."

In the White House, Thomas Jefferson

dressed very simply. He wore slippers and plain clothes. He looked like a farmer walking around in his riding britches. The ladies of Washington were disappointed. When John Adams was president, they were invited to fancy teas. They called on Jefferson to ask him to have teas every morning. He refused to do so. There were no tea parties for society when he was in office. The White House was disappointing to aristocratic visitors also. The roof leaked. The furniture was shabby

and worn. Jefferson bought some plain chairs to replace them. But the White House was a very happy place. Patsy and Polly visited their father and brought their children. Jefferson's sisters and the Carr children also visited. They stayed for long periods of time. Their happy laughter could be heard all over the White House lawn.

The people of the United States were delighted with Thomas Jefferson. This plain, simple man was a great hero to them. They wanted to celebrate his birthday as a national holiday. Jefferson refused.

"Let's celebrate July Fourth," he suggested. "That was the birthday of our country."

Many Federalists became jealous of Thomas Jefferson's popularity. New Englanders also became dissatisfied. Some even threatened to leave the Union.

"We're tired of being ruled by Virginians," they said. But other New Englanders pointed out that Jefferson was not just a Virginian. He was an American, and a great one at that.

Jefferson could be stern, too. When Spain

turned New Orleans over to France, Jefferson went into action.

"We cannot tolerate a tyrant like Napoleon controlling the mouth of the Mississippi," he said.

Some people called for war. Jefferson shook his head. "One war in our generation was enough," he said. "I'll send James Monroe to France to buy New Orleans."

James Monroe and Robert Livingston, our Minister to France, did more. They bought all of the Louisiana Territory for fifteen million dollars. It was the biggest bargain in our history. The territory was twice the size of the original colonies. Jefferson sent Lewis and Clark on an expedition to explore the new territory. They were instructed to find a way to the Pacific coast.

A terrible tragedy again darkened Thomas Jefferson's life. His daughter Polly died. Thomas Jefferson rushed back to Monticello to attend the funeral. He grieved for a long time.

Aaron Burr ran for governor of New York

while still vice-president of the United States. Alexander Hamilton aided DeWitt Clinton, who became the governor. Burr became very angry. He challenged Hamilton to a duel and shot him to death. Thomas Jefferson was greatly shocked to hear this news.

"Hamilton was a brilliant man and a loyal American," he said. "Death has removed a person our country cannot afford to lose." Jefferson suspected Aaron Burr of disloyalty. There were ugly rumors that Burr wanted to set up a southwest empire with himself as king.

In 1804 Jefferson was elected President again. DeWitt Clinton became the Vice-President. The government of the people, for the people, and by the people was proving more popular than rule by the privileged few.

Jefferson made no speeches or campaign promises, but the people trusted him. He was their champion, the friend of liberty. When Aaron Burr tried to set up his kingdom in Texas, Jefferson had him arrested.

"He's a dangerous man," he said, "and a
178

threat to the safety of the country."

Aaron Burr was tried for treason. There wasn't enough evidence against him, and he was freed. However, public opinion was against him. He left the country after his trial and didn't return for several years.

Serious trouble now developed for the United States. France and England declared war on each other. Each tried to stop the United States from trading with the other. The English boarded American ships, dragged off innocent sailors, and forced them to serve on their English ships. A war spirit flamed through the United States. Jefferson refused to listen. He tried to avoid war by passing the Embargo Act. This meant that Americans were forbidden to trade with foreign countries. The law caused a great lack of money. Factories shut down. Farmers could not sell their products to foreign markets. Businesses failed. Many people were out of work.

Jefferson received the blame for this. People wrote him bitter, insulting letters.

Newspapers criticized him. Although Jefferson did not like this, he defended the people's right to criticize him.

"As long as a citizen is free to speak his mind, our essential freedoms are safe," he said.

In spite of the bad times, the people wanted Thomas Jefferson to run for a third term as President in 1808. He refused. "Eight years are enough for one man to be in office," he told his supporters.

Finally, Congress repealed the Embargo Act. "It caused us great difficulty," Jefferson said, "but it kept us out of war. That's a small price to pay to prevent slaughter."

In the presidential campaign, Jefferson backed James Madison and DeWitt Clinton as President and Vice-President. They were elected. Jefferson was happy.

"James Madison is a good man," he said. "Our country will be safe under his leadership."

His daughter Patsy came to the White House to help him move. They put all his

notes and his records in thirty boxes. Only twenty-nine boxes arrived at Monticello. The most important one, his studies on the Indian languages and customs, was almost entirely destroyed. Jefferson was upset. A lifetime of research was lost forever. Now that he was finally free to retire, he wanted to devote time to his Indian studies. He wanted to discover where the Indians came from. He wanted to know more about their languages.

"Oh, well," he sighed. "It was not meant to be. Some day, someone will discover the truth about our Indian friends."

Jefferson never lost his interest in science. Even though he had never discovered any mammoth bones, he was partly responsible for the discovery of an entire mammoth skeleton. Just before his first term as President, Jefferson had loaned some Navy pumps to an American scientist, Charles Willson Peale. With the aid of the pumps, Peale had discovered the mammoth in a swamp near Peekskill, New York. Tom was pleased.

"This proves that the story of the big buffalo, which was told to me many years ago by Chief Ontassete, is true," Tom said. He would have worked with Peale if the discovery hadn't been made just at the time when he could go to Monticello and spend his life doing the things he had always wanted to do. He shook hands with James Madison at the White House.

"Good-by, James," he said gleefully. "Even though I am sixty-six years old, I feel like a schoolboy released from school on a holiday."

CHAPTER 16

"Master Jefferson Is Back!"

As soon as James Madison's inauguration was over, Jefferson left by carriage for his home on the mountain. A raging snow storm developed between Washington and Virginia. He left his carriage and rode on horseback for three days. It reminded him of the time he had brought his new bride to the honeymoon cottage. He sighed deeply. "There has been much sadness since then," he thought.

At the foot of the mountain, he was greeted by his daughter, son-in-law, grandchildren, and all the servants and slaves. They were overjoyed at the sight of their beloved leader.

"Master Jefferson is back!" the slaves

shouted joyfully. They loved Master Tom.
He always treated them so kindly.

The years that followed were happy years
for Jefferson. He spent much time perfect-
ing his inventions and working on new ones.
He put his cannon-ball clock in perfect order. It still runs. He invented a dumb-
waiter, and his bed that pulled into the
ceiling still fascinates visitors. He also invented a folding ladder which was many
years ahead of its time. He kept on building
and beautifying Monticello until it became
one of the finest houses in the New World.

During the War of 1812 against the British
the Library of Congress was destroyed. Jefferson offered his own splendid library to his
country.

"Pay me what you think it is worth," he
told the Congressmen.

Congress paid him only half of what the
library cost him. Jefferson didn't complain.

"I will start building a new library," he
said. "I cannot live without books."

One thing had always bothered Jefferson.

186

His Congressional bill for general education had never been passed. "I know some day it will be the law of the land," he said. "But I would like to do something for the education of our youth before I die."

The chance came. Jefferson and some other men planned to build a university in Charlottesville. They were going to call it Center College, but Jefferson saw a chance to have it accepted as the official university of Virginia. He called a meeting of the twenty-four leading citizens of the state. They all came. The President of the United States, James Monroe, attended. So did a former President, James Madison, as well as leading judges, lawyers, and statesmen. Jefferson drew a map. He argued that Charlottesville was the best place for the new university. Other men backed their own towns, such as Staunton and Richmond.

Jefferson's map decided the issue. He received sixteen votes for Charlottesville. He was appointed the first rector of the university. It was his job to work out the building plan, decide on the studies, and hire the faculty. Jefferson was greatly pleased. He rose to his feet with his eyes shining.

"This is the work I love, gentlemen. I'll do my best."

"That will be better than any other man in the world can do," said James Madison, and James Monroe heartily agreed.

He worked hard on his new project. He drew plans for the red brick buildings. He still admired Palladio, the great Italian architect. But he also put many of his own original ideas in the drawings. He remembered all the fine buildings he had seen in London, Paris, and other cities of Europe. He took the best features of all for his college.

The cornerstone of the first building was laid in 1817. Jefferson had a special telescope on Monticello, so he could watch the progress of the work. He spent days at a time watching through the glass.

In 1824, General Lafayette visited Thomas Jefferson at Monticello. The old friends had a wonderful reunion. They talked about

188

the dark days when the English invaded
Virginia while Jefferson was governor. They
discussed their days in France. But Jefferson
did more than talk. He used his influence in
Congress to have Congress vote Lafayette two
hundred thousand dollars.

"It is a small amount to pay Lafayette for
his loyal service to our country," he said.

Thomas Jefferson was a generous host to
the thousands who visited him. Patsy often
protested.

"Father, there are fifty people who want to
stay over and have dinner," she said. "We
can't take care of them all."

"Find a place for them," her father answered. "Feed them our best food. I have
never turned anyone away, and I never will."

Because of his generosity, Jefferson became bankrupt. He was discouraged, thinking that now he would have to sell Monticello
to pay his debts. The people of the United
States came rushing to his aid.

"We will not let this happen to our great
Jefferson," they said. They collected twenty

thousand dollars, and they saved Monticello.

On May 7, 1825, the University of Virginia opened its doors. Jefferson was almost eighty-two years old. "My work is nearing an end," he said. "I am content."

On July 4, 1826, fifty years from the day his Declaration of Independence was accepted, the grand old man died peacefully.

"I hear the bells ringing," were his last words. And he did hear the bells of the whole United States ringing to celebrate the country's freedom.

So at the age of eighty-three, Thomas Jefferson finally ceased to serve his country. He was the greatest genius of his time. He was a lawyer, architect, musician, botanist, farmer, writer, philosopher, and politician. He had designed Monticello, the Capitol at Richmond, and the University of Virginia. And he had helped plan Washington, D.C. But he was proudest of the free government of the people, for the people, and by the people, which he had created. Because of Thomas Jefferson's genius, life, liberty, and the pursuit of happiness were guaranteed in this country for all time. He was truly the friend and champion of the people.

On his gravestone were inscribed the three achievements he cherished most.

Here was buried
Thomas Jefferson
author
of the Declaration
of American Independence
of the Statute of Virginia
for religious freedom &
Father of the University
of Virginia

He was buried in the family plot on his mountain. Next to him was Dabney Carr. Thomas Jefferson had kept his promise that he and Dabney would some day be buried side by side on the mountain.

Many people visit Monticello. Some say they can almost see Thomas Jefferson, tall, stately, dignified, planning for the freedom of mankind.

Author's Note

Thomas Jefferson is often thought of as the greatest genius ever to have been born and lived on the North American continent. He was many years ahead of his time in his thinking and in his contributions to our country. One can't help wondering what additional miracles he might have accomplished if he could have spent all of his time on just one of his talents — either as a writer, naturalist, musician, architect, or scientist!

Yet, the fifty years he spent in political life produced the greatest gift of all . . . freedom for the common man. He was the first to assure the people by law and in writing that freedom would always be theirs in America. My father, and millions like him, traveled halfway around the world to share this precious freedom.

JOSEPH OLGIN